Achieving TABE® Success in Reading

in Reading

Level M

D1305817

Wright Group

Executive Editor: Linda Kwil
Marketing Manager: Sean Klunder
Production Manager: Genevieve Kelley
Cover Designer: Vickie Tripp

 **Wright Group**

ISBN: 0-07-704460-6

Send all inquiries to:
Wright Group/McGraw-Hill
130 East Randolph Street, Suite 400
Chicago, IL 60601

Manufactured in the United States of America.

10 11 MAL 12 11 10

The **McGraw·Hill** Companies

Table of Contents

Table of Contents

To the Learner

If reading has never been easy for you, Contemporary's *Achieving TABE Success in Reading* will help. The workbook will explain basic comprehension skills. The reader will let you practice those skills on a short, interesting story. *Achieving TABE Success in Reading* will build your confidence in your ability to read.

Using Contemporary's *Achieving TABE Success in Reading* is a good way to improve your reading comprehension skills. The workbook covers
- vocabulary
- recalling information
- using graphic information
- constructing meaning
- extending meaning

Included in the workbook are a Pretest and a Posttest. The Pretest will help you find your reading strengths and weaknesses. Then you can use the workbook lessons to improve your skills. When you have finished the lessons and exercises, the Posttest will help you see if you have mastered those skills. Usually mastery means completing 80% of the questions correctly.

Achieving TABE Success in Reading will help you develop specific reading skills. Each workbook is self-contained with the Answer Key at the back of the book. Clear directions will guide you through the lessons and exercises.

Each lesson in the **workbook** is divided into four parts:

- The **first page** clearly defines, explains, and illustrates the skill. The examples prepare you for the work in the following exercises.

- **Practice** lets you work on the skill just introduced.

- **Apply** gives you a different way to practice the comprehension skill.

- **Check Up** provides a quick test on the skill covered in the lesson.

Each selection in the **reader** will let you practice reading. The article or story will grab your interest and keep you reading to the end. When you finish reading, you will

- check your understanding of the story

- apply the workbook lesson's skill to the story

How to Use This Workbook

1. Take the Pretest on pages 7–15. Check your answers with the Answer Key on page 16. Refer to the Evaluation Chart on page 16 to find the skills on which you need to work.

2. Take each four-page lesson one at a time. Ask your teacher for help with any problems you have.

3. Use the Answer Key, which begins on page 224, to correct your answers after each exercise.

4. At the end of each unit, complete the Review and Assessment. These will check your progress. After the Assessment, your teacher may want to discuss your answers with you.

5. At the end of some lessons, you will see a Read On note about a selection in the reader for *Achieving TABE Success in Reading*. Take a break from the workbook and read the story or article. Answer the comprehension questions and the skill questions at the end of the story.

6. After you have finished all five units, take the Posttest on pages 217–222. Check your answers on page 223. Then discuss your progress with your teacher.

Pretest

Circle the word that is spelled correctly and best completes each sentence.

1. The _____ of the high school recently retired.

   A principal

   B principle

   C princeple

   D principul

2. _____ the first person to arrive.

   F You're

   G Yure

   H Your

   J Yeer

3. Our _____ had never been to the art museum.

   A visitir

   B visiter

   C visitar

   D visitor

4. After reading the critic's _____, I decided to go to see the movie.

   F reiview

   G review

   H reevue

   J reveiw

Circle the answer that is a synonym for the underlined word.

5. original <u>thought</u>

  A paragraph

  B idea

  C painting

  D speech

6. <u>anxious</u> to get started

  F reluctant

  G frightened

  H eager

  J happy

7. <u>tie</u> the string to the balloon

  A cut

  B fasten

  C tangle

  D clamp

8. cooling <u>wind</u> from the south

  F cloud

  G storm

  H weather

  J breeze

9. <u>repair</u> the broken window

  A fix

  B return

  C discard

  D build

10. <u>ache</u> in her side

  F disease

  G pain

  H remedy

  J medicine

Read the index for _Understanding Thomas Jefferson_ and circle the answer to each question.

11. On what page would you find a photograph of the Declaration of Independence?

  A 43

  B 221

  C 224

  D 186

12. Which of these entries is discussed at greatest length?

  F national debt

  G Declaration of Independence

  H Delawares

  J Democratic Party

Circle the answer that is an antonym for the underlined word.

13. <u>scorching</u> summer day

    A tropical

    B freezing

    C warm

    D humid

14. <u>superior</u> team

    F inferior

    G best

    H experienced

    J lazy

15. <u>repel</u> insects

    A replace

    B attract

    C resist

    D produce

16. <u>humble</u> person

    F modest

    G meek

    H proud

    J quiet

17. shirt with a <u>tight</u> weave

    A loose

    B light

    C heavy

    D cool

18. <u>high</u> price

    F unfair

    G low

    H tall

    J costly

Circle the answer for each question.

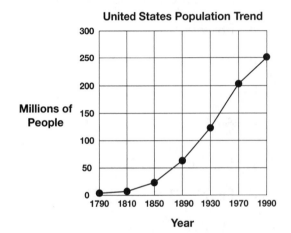

19. What do the vertical lines on the graph indicate?

    A number of people

    B percentage of people

    C years

    D miles

20. In what year was the population about 25,000,000?

    F 1810

    G 1850

    H 1890

    J 1970

Read the flight schedule and answer the questions.

Flight	City of Origin	Scheduled Arrival	Arrival Time	Gate
221	Dallas	10:30 A.M.	10:45 A.M.	B12
237	Seattle	11:05 A.M.	11:05 A.M.	B8
306	New York	11:25 A.M.	11:30 A.M.	B10
316	Omaha	1:15 P.M.	1:50 P.M.	C18
321	Atlanta	2:00 P.M.	2:30 P.M.	A12

21. At what gate did Flight 306 arrive?

A B8

B B10

C C18

D A12

22. Which flight was 30 minutes late?

F Flight 221

G Flight 237

H Flight 306

J Flight 321

23. Where did Flight 237 originate?

A Atlanta

B New York

C Omaha

D Seattle

24. Which flight was on time?

F Flight 306

G Flight 221

H Flight 237

J Flight 321

Circle the answer for each question.

25. What information would **not** be asked for on a credit card application?

A bank name

B checking account number

C shipping address

D other credit card numbers

26. What information would be asked for on a job application?

F spouse's name

G experience

H billing address

J savings account number

Read the passages and answer the questions.

Sometimes gardening and self-defense go hand in hand. That is true in the case of the spider crab. The spider crab is a saltwater species that lives on the sea bottom. The little crab cultivates a garden of seaweed on its own shell. First it snips some small pieces of seaweed. Then it arranges the pieces carefully on its shell. The plants take root and soon they cover the whole crab. From then on, the spider crab can hide from its enemies under its own garden.

27. As used in this paragraph, *cultivate* means

   A hide

   B develop by training

   C plant and grow

   D trap

28. From this paragraph, you can conclude that

   F the spider crab is a creature that hides with the help of camouflage

   G the spider crab spins a web in the water

   H spider crabs can be found in gardens

   J the spider crab's enemies are afraid of plants

29. Where does the spider crab live?

   A on sandy beaches

   B in saltwater

   C in the garden

   D in lakes

30. What does the spider crab do before it arranges the seaweed on its shell?

   F hides from its enemies

   G burrows in the sand

   H cultivates a seaweed garden

   J snips small pieces of seaweed

They're known as white dwarfs. They are a type of small star. At one time, these stars were huge and red. They were known as supernovas. Supernovas eventually collapse in upon themselves. What remains is a much smaller star with all the weight of the larger one. In fact, some white dwarfs are about 36 times as dense as water. That means that one cubic inch would weigh about 650 tons.

31. What is the main idea of this paragraph?

   A White dwarfs were once huge, red stars.

   B Some stars are smaller than other stars.

   C White dwarfs are small but incredibly dense stars.

   D Stars are more dense than water.

32. A piece of a dwarf star the size of a pea would be

   F too small to be measured

   G too heavy for the strongest person to lift

   H too bright to look at

   J too small to be seen without a microscope

33. The author's purpose in this paragraph is to

   A persuade the reader to learn more about stars

   B inform the reader about the best time to see star formations

   C tell a story about supernovas

   D describe white dwarfs

If you are like most people, you just jump in the shower and wash your hair daily. Well, you can have stronger, better-looking hair by knowing a few simple facts about shampooing. If you shampoo every day, you could be hurting your hair. All that scrubbing breaks and splits hair shafts. Skin doctors say you should skip some days. Wash your hair gently, starting with a gentle scalp massage. Be careful not to rub too hard. And you don't have to buy expensive products that have protein and vitamins added to them. Doctors say hair cannot be nourished from the outside. Don't stick to one brand either. With repeated use, a shampoo becomes less and less effective.

34. From this paragraph, you can generalize that

    F   hair never has to be washed

    G   everyone's hair is much stronger than people think

    H   everyone should change their shampoo occasionally

    J   no one has healthy hair

35. Why is buying expensive hair products a waste of money?

    A   because hair cannot be nourished from the outside

    B   because it is better to go to a skin doctor for help with your hair

    C   because scrubbing breaks the hair shafts

    D   because your hair only needs to be washed once a week

36. According to this paragraph, what will be the likely outcome if you cut back to washing your hair every other day?

    F   Your hair will get greasy.

    G   Your scalp will start to flake.

    H   You'll have fewer split ends.

    J   You'll have a buildup of shampoo.

The giraffe and the mouse seem to have nothing in common, aside from both being animals. The mouse is a tiny creature. Most mice never grow to be more than a few inches long. Giraffes, on the other hand, are huge. A giraffe's neck alone is from 7 to 10 feet long. Yet, in one way they are just alike. It is their necks that the mouse and giraffe have in common. The necks of both are made up of small bones called vertebrae. Though they differ greatly in size, the mouse and the giraffe have the same number of vertebrae in their necks.

37. This paragraph is about the

    A differences between giraffes and mice

    B number of bones in a giraffe's neck

    C ways in which mice and giraffes are alike and different

    D size of mice

38. How big is a giraffe?

    F a few inches

    G 7 feet

    H 10 feet

    J not stated

39. What is the author's tone in this passage?

    A amused

    B sentimental

    C matter of fact

    D sarcastic

Why is it called a sandwich? The sandwich was named for the man who is thought to have been the first to eat meat between two slices of bread. His name was John Montagu, fourth Earl of Sandwich. Montagu liked to do things in a big way. He used to host 48-hour-long card games. The earl would ask his servant to slip some meat between two pieces of bread and hand it to him. Many people thought this was bad table manners. But it caught on among card players. Sandwiches became common at other informal meals.

40. Which is the best paraphrase of this paragraph?

   F John Montagu liked to eat while playing cards. Sometimes the card games lasted 48 hours. Many other card players ate while they played.

   G The sandwich was named after John Montagu, the Earl of Sandwich. Montagu used to host long card games. His servant gave him slices of meat on bread to eat during the card games. Soon sandwiches became popular at informal meals.

   H The sandwich was invented to eat during card games. Some people thought this was rude.

   J John Montagu put meat between bread.

41. Which sentence is **not** a fact?

   A John Montagu was the fourth Earl of Sandwich.

   B Montagu used to host 48-hour-long card games.

   C Eating sandwiches at card game tables is bad manners.

   D Sandwiches became common at other informal meals.

42. Which of the following caused sandwiches to become popular?

   F They were invented by a nobleman.

   G Gamblers liked to have a hand free while eating.

   H Young people liked them because they were seen as rude.

   J Formal meals were becoming less common.

43. Which words best describe John Montagu?

   A shy and quiet

   B lazy and irresponsible

   C fun-loving and intense

   D rude and unkind

Pretest Answer Key and Evaluation Chart

This Pretest has been designed to help you determine which reading skills you need to study. This chart shows which skill is being covered with each test question. Circle the questions you answered incorrectly and go to the practice pages in this book covering those skills. Carefully work through all the practice pages before taking the Posttest.

Key

1.	A
2.	F
3.	D
4.	G
5.	B
6.	H
7.	B
8.	J
9.	A
10.	G
11.	C
12.	F
13.	B
14.	F
15.	B
16.	H
17.	A
18.	G
19.	C
20.	G
21.	B
22.	J
23.	D
24.	H
25.	C
26.	G
27.	C
28.	F
29.	B
30.	J
31.	C
32.	G
33.	D
34.	H
35.	A
36.	H
37.	C
38.	J
39.	C
40.	G
41.	C
42.	G
43.	C

Tested Skills	Question Numbers	Practice Pages
synonyms	5, 6, 7, 8, 9, 10	21–24, 25–28
antonyms	13, 14, 15, 16, 17, 18	29–32, 33–36
context clues	27	37–40, 41–44
spelling	1, 2, 3, 4	45–48, 49–52
details	29, 38	59–62, 63–66
sequence	30	67–70, 71–74
stated concepts	32	75–78, 79–82
graphs	19, 20	89–92
schedules	21, 22, 23, 24	101–104
forms/consumer materials	25, 26	97–100, 109–112, 113–116
indexes	11, 12	105–108
character traits	43	123–126, 127–130
main idea	31	131–134, 135–138
compare and contrast	37	139–142, 143–146
drawing conclusions	28	147–150, 151–154
cause and effect	42	155–158, 159–162
summary and paraphrase	40	163–166
predicting outcomes	36	177–180, 181–184
fact and opinion	41	185–188, 189–192
author's purpose	33	193–196
author's effect and intention	39	197–200
generalizations	34	201–204
applying passage elements	35	209–212

Correlation Chart

Correlations Between Contemporary's Instructional Materials and TABE® Reading

Subskill	TABE® Form 9	TABE® Form 10	TABE® Survey 9	TABE® Survey 10	Practice and Instruction Pages			
					Achieving TABE Success in Reading, Level M*	Essentials of Reading (4 & 5)**	On the Edge: In Your Dreams	On the Edge: Scared Stiff
Interpret Graphic Information								
index		49, 50		24, 25	W: 105–108 R: 50–56			
graphs	49, 50		24, 25		W: 89–92 R: 37–43			
forms	36, 38	35, 36	14	16, 17	W: 97–104 R: 44–49	4: 47–48, 103–104 5: 55–56, 103–104		
consumer materials	31		9		W: 109–116 R: 50–56	4: 57–58, 85–86 5: 65–66, 75–76		
Words in Context								
same meaning	27, 30, 37	4, 10, 14, 40	6, 8, 13	3, 7, 21	W: 21–28 R: 5–10, 11–16	4: 15, 33, 53, 63, 73, 99 5: 7, 25, 71, 99, 109	8, 20, 21, 32, 56, 68, 80, 81, 92, 104, 116	8, 9, 20, 32, 44, 56, 68, 69, 80, 92, 104, 116
opposite meaning	33	25, 41	10	12	W: 29–36 R: 5–10	4: 15, 33, 53, 81 5: 7, 25, 109	9	21
Recall Information								
details	8, 14, 22, 23, 42	2, 3, 15, 16, 23, 37	4, 18	8, 10, 18	W: 59–66 R: 22–26	4: 27–28, 36, 55, 66, 113 5: 9–10, 19–20, 27, 36, 46, 64, 93–94, 111	10, 34, 94	10, 22, 34, 94
sequence	7, 9, 26, 32	7, 12, 31, 39		1, 5, 20	W: 67–74 R: 27–32	4: 65, 102 5: 10, 28, 46, 111	7, 15, 22, 27, 51, 82, 115	15, 22, 27, 34, 63
stated concepts	2, 40, 46, 48	5, 6, 45	16, 21, 23		W: 75–82 R: 33–36	4: 17, 66, 76 5: 45, 74, 84	39, 118	99
Construct Meaning								
character aspects		32, 44		23	W: 121, 123–130 R: 57–62	4: 27, 83 5: 10, 28, 35 46, 73, 101	75, 103	3, 15, 19, 55, 63, 87, 103, 111
main idea	1, 12, 19, 29, 35, 45	1, 9, 43	1, 12, 20		W: 131–138 R: 57–62	4: 46, 76, 84, 94 5: 45, 54, 84, 94, 102	10, 94	10, 94

Subskill	TABE® Form 9	TABE® Form 10	TABE® Survey 9	TABE® Survey 10	Practice and Instruction Pages			
					*Achieving TABE Success in Reading, Level M**	*Essentials of Reading (4 & 5)***	*On the Edge: In Your Dreams*	*On the Edge: Scared Stiff*
summary/ paraphrase	10, 41	20, 29, 48	17		W: 163–166 R: 68–72	4: 10, 18, 36, 55, 66, 76, 94 5: 18, 64, 74, 93–94, 102	3, 7, 15, 19, 22, 27, 31, 39, 43, 51, 55, 63, 67, 70, 75, 79, 87, 91, 99,103, 105, 111, 115	3, 7, 15, 19, 22, 27, 31, 39, 43, 51, 55, 63, 67, 70, 75, 79, 87, 91, 99, 103, 111, 115
cause/effect	20	11, 42	2	4, 22	W: 155–162 R: 68–72	4: 10, 17, 28, 46, 65, 84 5: 18, 35–36, 73	3, 15, 27, 31, 43, 51, 63, 79, 91, 103, 111	3, 7, 15, 19, 27, 31, 39, 43, 51, 55, 63, 67, 75, 79, 91, 99, 103
compare/ contrast	13, 34	17, 21, 34, 47	11	9, 15	W: 122, 139–146 R: 63–67	4: 17, 55, 65, 76, 101 5: 63, 110	34, 46, 63, 93, 117	33, 46, 82, 93, 103, 115, 118
conclusion	43	13, 22, 46		6	W: 147–154 R: 63–67		3, 11, 15, 23, 31, 39, 43, 63, 71, 95, 115	3, 11, 23, 35, 39, 79, 87, 91, 95, 111, 119
supporting evidence	3, 28		7		W: 167–170 R: 68–72	4: 94–95, 101, 113 5: 53, 83	3, 7, 15, 19, 27, 31, 39, 43, 51, 55, 59, 63, 67, 75, 79, 87, 91, 99, 103, 107, 111, 115	3, 7, 15, 19, 27, 31, 39, 43, 51, 55, 59, 63, 67, 75, 79, 83, 87, 91, 99, 103 111, 115

Evaluate/Extend Meaning

Subskill	TABE® Form 9	TABE® Form 10	TABE® Survey 9	TABE® Survey 10	*Achieving TABE Success in Reading, Level M**	*Essentials of Reading (4 & 5)***	*On the Edge: In Your Dreams*	*On the Edge: Scared Stiff*
fact/opinion	4, 39	8	15	2	W: 185–192 R: 73–77	4: 9, 18, 27, 45, 75, 93 5: 17, 27, 101, 110	35, 47, 59	47, 59, 83, 103, 107
predict outcomes	11	33			W: 177–184 R: 73–77	4: 9, 35, 101 5: 9, 35, 53, 63, 93, 110	27, 67, 83, 99, 119	23, 71
apply passage elements	15, 47	24, 27, 38	22	11, 14, 19	W: 209–212 R: 85–89	4: 46, 55 5: 10, 45, 64, 84, 93	46	106
generalizations	5, 18, 25	26	5	13	W: 201–204 R: 78–84	4: 17, 18, 66, 76, 93–94 5: 9, 27–28, 73	35, 67, 79, 87, 103, 107, 111, 119	11, 47, 71, 91, 107
effect/ intention	16, 17, 21, 44	30	3, 19		W: 197–200 R: 78–84	4: 83, 113	95, 106	23, 31, 35, 95
author purpose	6, 24	18, 28			W:175,193–196 R: 78–84	4: 75	23, 58, 95, 106	23, 35, 51, 58, 95
style techniques		19			W: 176, 205–208 R: 85–89		81, 93, 117	33, 69, 93

* W = Workbook; R = Reader.

** 4 = Book 4; 5 = Book 5.

TABE® Forms 9 and 10 are published by CTB/McGraw-Hill. TABE is a registered trademark of The McGraw-Hill Companies.

Health Watch

What do you know about health words? Look at the list of
health words. Each relates to a different part of physical health.
Write the word under the correct heading.

calories	immunity	respiratory
food pyramid	exercise	allergy
cardiovascular	protein	energy
vaccination	antibodies	vitamins
agility	bacteria	fiber

Physical Fitness	**Healthful Eating**	**Disease**
_____	_____	_____
_____	_____	_____
_____	_____	_____
_____	_____	_____
_____	_____	_____

Were you familiar with all the words? Use a group of words. Write a paragraph that
explains how you keep physically fit.

_____

_____

_____

_____

_____

_____

_____

Blends and Clips

Some words are **blends** of other words.

    smoke + fog = smog

    modulator + demodulator = modem

Combine each pair of words to make a blend. Write a sentence using the blend.

1. breakfast + lunch = _____

_____

2. cheese + hamburger = _____

_____

3. motor + hotel = _____

_____

4. information + commercial = _____

_____

Some words are **clips**, or shortened forms, of words.

    saxophone   sax

    automobile   auto

Shorten each word to make a clip. Write a sentence using the clip.

5. gasoline _____

_____

6. influenza _____

_____

7. photograph _____

_____

8. moving pictures _____

_____

Recognizing Synonyms

Read the following words: below   under   beneath
These words all have similar meanings.
Words with similar, or almost the same, meanings are called **synonyms.** Look for synonyms in this sentence.

I love my new car, but my son prefers his old automobile.

Car and *automobile* are synonyms.

Find the word in the box that is a synonym for each numbered word.

show	need	tale	brief	top
children	small	unlock	attempt	twist

1. demonstrate _____

2. require _____

3. crest _____

4. youngsters _____

5. story _____

6. tiny _____

7. try _____

8. open _____

9. short _____

10. turn _____

Write a synonym for each underlined word. Use words from the list above.

11. The glass blowers will <u>demonstrate</u> their craft. _____

12. Mr. Salazar read a <u>tale</u> to his son. _____

13. I'll <u>try</u> to attend the event, but I'm not sure I can. _____

14. <u>Turn</u> the cap to open the bottle. _____

15. All people <u>require</u> food and shelter. _____

16. I tried to <u>unlock</u> the door with the wrong key! _____

17. Hummingbirds build very <u>small</u> nests. _____

18. The climbers finally reached the <u>top</u> of the mountain. _____

19. The playground is ideal for the <u>children</u>. _____

20. The book cover gives a <u>short</u> summary of the story. _____

Practice

Find a synonym in this box for each underlined word below.

arrives	melody	grand	majority	pursue
roam	go	mountains	picked	females

1. It sounds as if the <u>hills</u> are singing.

   _____

2. <u>Wander</u> through the mountains of West Virginia.

   _____

3. You may hear a banjo being <u>plucked</u> and strummed.

   _____

4. Chances are that the <u>tune</u> is not coming from a radio.

   _____

5. <u>Follow</u> the sound, and you may find a woman picking tunes on a banjo.

   _____

6. When winter <u>comes</u>, she won't put the banjo away.

   _____

7. The woman will <u>move</u> into the warm kitchen.

   _____

8. Many West Virginian <u>women</u> have been playing instruments for generations.

   _____

9. Few of them can read music, and <u>most</u> are self-taught.

   _____

10. It's all part of a <u>great</u> musical tradition.

    _____

Apply

Write a sentence using a synonym for the underlined word.

1. The world's <u>best</u> jumper will never go to the Olympics.

   _____

2. That's because this <u>great</u> jumper is a kangaroo.

   _____

3. The kangaroo lives in Australia's grasslands and <u>forests</u>.

   _____

4. The secret to the kangaroo's jumping ability is its <u>big</u> back feet.

   _____

5. Although an average kangaroo is no more than 70 inches tall, its back feet <u>might</u> be as long as 10 inches!

   _____

6. With these big back feet, a kangaroo can <u>jump</u> for hours at a time.

   _____

7. Sometimes a kangaroo will hop 20 miles without <u>resting</u>.

   _____

8. A kangaroo could easily <u>bound</u> over a parked car.

   _____

9. Kangaroos are <u>timid</u> and do not attack unless they are cornered.

   _____

10. A kangaroo's great speed is its best <u>defense</u>.

    _____

Check Up

Circle the synonym for each underlined word.

1. In Scotland, boys and girls are <u>called</u> laddies and lassies.

   A yelled

   B termed

   C understood

   D found

2. Lassie is also the name of the <u>world's</u> most famous collie.

   F nation's

   G country's

   H satellite's

   J earth's

3. Collies <u>originally</u> came from Scotland.

   A recently

   B finally

   C sometimes

   D first

4. They are large, <u>slender</u> dogs with long, soft fur.

   F stout

   G heavy

   H furry

   J slim

5. They have <u>gentle</u> eyes and long, narrow, pointed faces.

   A tender

   B brown

   C large

   D round

6. Collies make <u>good</u> house dogs and farm dogs.

   F kind

   G excellent

   H odd

   J peculiar

7. Owners find that collies can be taught <u>difficult</u> tricks.

   A hard

   B funny

   C easy

   D many

8. But collies are most <u>comfortable</u> out in the fields, tending sheep.

   F easy

   G friendly

   H satisfied

   J troublesome

Using Synonyms

You know that words with similar, or almost the same, meanings are **synonyms.**
Because synonyms do not have exactly the same meaning, sometimes two words can
be synonyms in one sentence but not in another. Find the synonyms in this sentence.

We took pictures at the picnic, and the photos were great.

Pictures and *photos* are synonyms in this sentence. You could use one or the other, and
the sentence would still have the same meaning.

Could *photos* be a synonym for *pictures* in the following sentence?

The artist painted beautiful pictures.

In this sentence, *photos* would not make sense in place of *pictures*.

**The words in each group below can be synonyms. Underline the two synonyms in each
sentence. Then write a new sentence that uses the remaining synonym in the group.**

make, build, construct	came, arrived, reached
dine, eat, devour	grab, take, steal
right, proper, correct	tiny, little, small

1. Although viruses are tiny, these little germs can make people very sick.

   _____

2. The company will build on that corner and construct a garage, too.

   _____

3. Let's grab some cookies and take them with us.

   _____

4. Wild animals devour their prey in order to eat.

   _____

5. The teacher will correct the papers to show all the right answers.

   _____

6. Don and Edna arrived at the same conclusion that Jim reached.

   _____

Practice

Write the best synonym to fit in each sentence.

1. Abraham Lincoln was famous for his storytelling and _____ sense of humor. (rapid, quick)

2. A member of Congress once visited the president during the

   _____ early days of the Civil War. (worried, troubled)

3. Lincoln began to tell an odd _____. (legend, story)

4. But it _____ that his guest was in no mood to hear it. (seemed, resembled)

5. He _____ to his feet and said, "Mr. President, I did not come here this morning to hear tales." (rose, ascended)

6. "It is too _____ a time," the guest said. (serious, thoughtful)

7. The smile _____ from Lincoln's face. (evaporated, vanished)

8. He replied, "Sit down, sir. I _____ you as an earnest and sincere man." (respect, idolize)

9. "You cannot be more anxious than I am _____," Lincoln continued. (loyal, constant)

10. "I say to you now that if it weren't for this occasional _____, I would die." (exit, vent)

Apply

Write a sentence using a synonym for each underlined word.

1. The Cape Cod Canal cuts the <u>sea</u> route between Boston and New York by seventy miles.

   _____

2. It also lets <u>ships</u> avoid sandbars off Cape Cod.

   _____

3. Those <u>shoals</u>, which sank many ships, got August Belmont started on the canal.

   _____

4. Belmont was a <u>wealthy</u> banker who sponsored the project in 1909.

   _____

5. It opened five years later as a toll <u>waterway</u>.

   _____

6. After 15 years, the United States government <u>bought</u> the canal.

   _____

7. To buy it and then <u>fix</u> it cost more than $30 million.

   _____

8. <u>Now</u> the canal is free, and ships no longer have to pay tolls.

   _____

9. It is wide enough to <u>allow</u> two-way traffic for all but the biggest ships.

   _____

10. Each year, thousands of boats <u>travel</u> through the Cape Cod Canal.

    _____

Check Up

Circle the synonym for each underlined word.

1. You have probably heard that no two snowflakes are <u>alike</u>.

   A different

   B complicated

   C the same

   D designed

2. It's an interesting fact, but how was it <u>discovered</u>?

   F found

   G invented

   H seen

   J considered

3. After all, snowflakes are small, and they melt very <u>quickly</u>.

   A quietly

   B silently

   C slowly

   D fast

4. In 1940 scientists came up with a way to <u>study</u> the structure of snowflakes.

   F change

   G examine

   H break

   J copy

5. They developed a chemical compound in which the <u>impression</u> of an actual snowflake can be left.

   A opinion

   B copy

   C suggestion

   D photograph

6. The <u>compound</u> is spread over a glass plate.

   F acid

   G paste

   H molecule

   J mixture

7. Snow falls onto the compound, which hardens around the <u>tiny</u> flakes.

   A frozen

   B beautiful

   C small

   D white

8. When the flakes melt and <u>dry up</u>, scientists can study their structures from the impressions left in the compound.

   F appear

   G evaporate

   H freeze

   J fall

Recognizing Antonyms

Words that are opposite in meaning are **antonyms**.

We mow the lawn in summer.
We shovel the snow in winter.

Summer and *winter* are antonyms.

Match each word with an antonym. Write the letter on the line.

_____	1. no one	**A**	funny
_____	2. cold	**B**	rejected
_____	3. noisy	**C**	everyone
_____	4. new	**D**	Northern
_____	5. serious	**E**	hot
_____	6. dangerous	**F**	safe
_____	7. understandable	**G**	old
_____	8. accepted	**H**	quiet
_____	9. destroyed	**I**	mysterious
_____	10. Southern	**J**	built

Complete each sentence with an antonym for the underlined word. Use words from the above list.

11. Canada is in the <u>Northern</u> Hemisphere; Argentina is in the _____ Hemisphere.

12. I bought a <u>new</u> television to replace the _____ one.

13. The school was <u>built</u> after the old one was _____.

14. <u>No one</u> came to the party because _____ was out of town.

15. A glass of _____ lemonade tastes good on a <u>hot</u> day.

16. People throughout the <u>quiet</u> library could hear the _____ children.

Practice

Choose an antonym for each numbered word and write it on the line.

1. receive

   take   give   purchase   _____

2. wonderful

   fantastic   great   horrible   _____

3. enemy

   foe   neighbor   friend   _____

4. catch

   hit   throw   play   _____

5. boring

   dull   entertaining   long   _____

6. follow

   lead   imitate   copy   _____

7. open

   uncover   remove   wrap   _____

8. slender

   slim   straight   thick   _____

9. talk

   shout   whisper   listen   _____

10. trust

   doubt   accept   believe   _____

Apply

Write a sentence using an antonym for each underlined word.

1. The world is <u>full</u> of plants.

   _____

2. There are thousands of <u>different</u> plants.

   _____

3. Some are <u>huge</u> trees, some are small garden plants, and others, such as algae, are microscopic.

   _____

4. Plants grow almost <u>everywhere</u> in the world.

   _____

5. Africa and South America have dense rain forests with <u>rare</u> plants most people have never seen.

   _____

6. The rain forests are so filled with trees, flowers, and vines that the sunlight barely reaches the forest <u>floor</u>.

   _____

7. Even in Antarctica, where it is <u>always</u> freezing cold, some plants have managed to grow.

   _____

8. But the place that has the <u>most</u> plants in the world isn't on any of these continents.

   _____

9. The <u>fact</u> is it's not on land at all.

   _____

10. Eighty-five percent of the world's plants <u>live</u> in the ocean!

   _____

Check Up

Circle the antonym for each underlined word.

1. The music was for very <u>young</u> children.

   A little

   B old

   C small

   D new

2. The movie came out <u>after</u> the play.

   F behind

   G with

   H following

   J before

3. The <u>fastest</u> racers were from France.

   A quickest

   B biggest

   C slowest

   D nearest

4. We <u>seldom</u> go to a baseball game.

   F rarely

   G often

   H never

   J soon

5. I could only eat <u>part</u> of my dessert.

   A half

   B all

   C two-thirds

   D piece

6. The cars were parked in the <u>back</u> of the parking lot.

   F side

   G front

   H middle

   J rear

7. <u>Everything</u> in the room was in its place.

   A Anything

   B Object

   C Choice

   D Nothing

8. The head of the department is always <u>kind</u> to her employees.

   F nice

   G aware

   H cruel

   J encouraging

Using Antonyms

Read the following words: on   off
These words have opposite meanings.
Two words that are opposite in meaning are called **antonyms**. Look
for the antonyms in this sentence.

      Jim's old shoes were so worn out he had to get new ones.

Old and *new* are antonyms.

Find the word in the box that is an antonym for each numbered word.

good	never	to	first	find
started	right	near	together	often

1. far   _____
2. from   _____
3. apart   _____
4. wrong   _____
5. seldom   _____

6. finished _____
7. always _____
8. lose _____
9. bad _____
10. last _____

Write an antonym for each underlined word to complete the sentence. Use words from the list above.

11. Marcela was <u>first</u> in the race, and Sarah was _____ .

12. We live pretty <u>far</u> from the stadium, but they live _____ it.

13. If I <u>lose</u> my keys, I know I'll never _____ them again.

14. Yoshi put the toaster <u>together</u> after it fell _____ .

15. Amanda got 90 answers <u>right</u> and 10 answers _____ .

16. Many runners <u>started</u> the race, but few _____ .

17. The girls promised <u>always</u> to be friends and _____ to part.

18. Sometimes a <u>bad</u> movie is fun, but I'd rather see a _____ movie.

19. Gerardo is leaving <u>from</u> Boston and going _____ Philadelphia.

Practice

Find an antonym in this box for each underlined word.

little	cause	friend	consider	smooth
negative	forget	aware	majority	hard

1. The seats in the theater were very <u>soft</u>.

   _____

2. It is easy to eat a <u>lot</u> at a buffet dinner.

   _____

3. The villain is the <u>enemy</u> of the hero.

   _____

4. Harsh weather can make your skin <u>rough</u>.

   _____

5. When you faint, you are <u>unconscious</u>.

   _____

6. The bill did not pass because only a <u>minority</u> voted for it.

   _____

7. Please <u>disregard</u> the notice you received in the mail.

   _____

8. Did Avery <u>remember</u> to pack warm clothes?

   _____

9. Protons are particles with <u>positive</u> charges.

   _____

10. The leaking pipes were one <u>effect</u> of poor maintenance.

   _____

Apply

Write a sentence using an antonym for each underlined word.

1. It looks like a <u>large</u>, black rubber disk.

   _____

2. The hockey puck has changed since the game <u>began</u>.

   _____

3. The <u>first</u> players used wooden balls from the game of cricket.

   _____

4. Then India rubber was brought to the <u>West</u>.

   _____

5. The bouncing rubber pucks made the game <u>faster</u> and more exciting.

   _____

6. However, the game became <u>wild</u> and unpredictable.

   _____

7. University students switched back to the <u>old</u> wooden balls.

   _____

8. Some players were still convinced that rubber was <u>better</u>.

   _____

9. <u>Finally</u>, a student cut the top and bottom off the ball and made a disk.

   _____

10. <u>After</u> that, hockey players started using the disks in their games.

   _____

Check Up

Circle the antonym for each underlined word.

1. Few sights are <u>more</u> spectacular than a total eclipse of the sun.

   A most

   B less

   C fewest

   D greater

2. During a solar eclipse, the sky <u>darkens</u> as the sun is slowly covered.

   F appears

   G soothes

   H lightening

   J lightens

3. Sometimes the sun resembles a <u>huge</u> black ball surrounded by a ring of fire.

   A enormous

   B shining

   C tiny

   D large

4. <u>Strange</u> as it may seem, solar eclipses are not caused by the sun.

   F familiar

   G curious

   H unusual

   J knowing

5. They occur when the moon moves <u>directly</u> between the sun and the earth.

   A quickly

   B indirectly

   C completely

   D unusually

6. The moon blots out much of the sun's <u>light</u> for a short time.

   F rays

   G brilliance

   H darkness

   J display

7. <u>Partial</u> solar eclipses take place fairly often.

   A total

   B somewhat

   C incomplete

   D huge

8. But total eclipses, in which the sun is completely <u>covered</u>, occur only about once every century.

   F discovered

   G recovered

   H undercover

   J uncovered

Read On   Read "Long Live Verdi!" As you read, look for synonyms and antonyms. Then answer the questions.

Recognizing Context Clues

To understand the meaning of an unfamiliar word, you can sometimes use **context clues**. These are clues or hints in the surrounding sentence or paragraph. Context clues can help you figure out what the word *misers* means in the following sentence.

> Both brothers were misers, people who hate to spend money on themselves or anyone else.

The sentence includes a group of words that defines *misers*. It tells you that misers are people who hate to spend money.

Use context clues to figure out the meaning of each underlined word. Then write the meaning on the line.

1. A person who feels <u>sluggish</u>, or tired, might complain of being "in the doldrums."

_____

2. But the <u>doldrums</u> are both a feeling and a place.

_____

3. The doldrums were discovered long ago, when sailors began to go out on the <u>high seas</u>—the open waters that belonged to no nation.

_____

4. There are certain places in the ocean near the equator where sailboats are often <u>stalled</u> because there is no wind to move them.

_____

5. If a sailboat enters this area, it can be <u>stranded</u> for days until wind fills its sails.

_____

6. Sailors learned long ago to <u>circumvent</u>, or avoid, these spots.

_____

7. They called these calm spots the <u>doldrums</u>.

_____

8. People who feel <u>listless</u>, or in a slump, often say they are "in the doldrums."

_____

Practice

Read the following passages. Then circle the answer for each question.

Talc is used to make powder for babies and adults. It <u>absorbs</u> water on the skin and provides it with oils. The <u>substance</u> comes from a rock called talc. When it is finely ground, talc feels soothing to the skin. Rock is not something you think of as being soft to the touch. But in the form of powder, talc provides a silky coat for your body after a bath.

1. To *absorb* is to

   A soak up

   B moisten

   C cover

   D spill

2. The word *substance* means

   F material

   G compound

   H mineral

   J oil

Parrots are known as birds that can talk. In fact, pet parrots can <u>mimic</u> the speech of humans. They can be taught to say anything their owners care to teach them. However, they can't learn to <u>express</u> their own ideas. They are merely imitators. So wild parrots never learn to talk.

3. To *mimic* is to

   A speak

   B imitate

   C learn

   D train

4. In this paragraph, *express* means

   F to create

   G to go rapidly

   H to stand for something else

   J to make known

Apply

Use context clues to figure out the meaning of the underlined word in each sentence or pair of sentences. Underline words or phrases that give you clues. Then circle the correct meaning of the word in the sentence.

1. Most birds flap their wings when they fly. But <u>soaring</u> birds can stay in the air for hours without moving their wings.

   A gliding   **B** falling   **C** flying

2. Condors, hawks, buzzards, and other soaring birds soar very much like an unmotorized airplane, or <u>glider</u>.

   F plane with no motor   **G** porch swing   **H** ice skater

3. Like gliders with <u>extended</u> wings, these birds keep their wings still and stretched out.

   A curled up   **B** pulled in   **C** spread open

4. They change directions by <u>slight</u>, or tiny, movements of the head, body, or tail.

   F very small   **G** trivial   **H** thin

5. They use moving air <u>currents</u> to rise and stay above the earth.

   A movements   **B** what's happening now   **C** downdrafts

6. Since air currents are <u>crucial</u> to soaring, soaring becomes impossible when the air is still.

   F helpful   **G** absolutely necessary   **H** useful

7. On windless days, soaring birds must either flap their wings like other birds or <u>hug</u> the earth.

   A stay close to   **B** squeeze   **C** put one's arms around

Check Up

Read the following passage. Then circle the answer for each question.

A fish out of water is soon dead, but a seal out of water is just plain clumsy. Seals are <u>amphibious mammals</u>. This means that they are warm-blooded, air-breathing creatures that live on land as well as in the water. In water, the seal is a <u>sleek</u>, or smooth, swimmer much like a fish. The seal's tube-shaped body <u>allows</u> it to glide, dart, and dive, making it a fine fisher. Its back feet are webbed like a duck's, and the seal uses them like a fish tail to <u>propel</u> itself swiftly forward. The seal's front limbs are <u>flippers</u>. In water the flippers allow the seal to quickly change direction. On land they merely <u>enable</u> the seal to drag itself forward. The seal's ancient <u>predecessors</u> were land creatures. Since their time, nature has redesigned the seal for living in water, too.

1. The phrase *amphibious mammals* means

   A animals that give birth to live young

   B warm-blooded, air-breathing creatures that live on land and in water

   C warm-blooded, air-breathing creatures

   D creatures that live in the water

2. In this passage, *sleek* means

   F shiny and glossy

   G smooth

   H elegant

   J slender

3. The word *propel* here means

   A pull

   B push

   C turn

   D flip

4. What are *flippers?*

   F a seal's feet

   G a seal's back limbs

   H a seal's tail

   J a seal's front limbs

5. The word *enable* means

   A make something possible

   B make something probable

   C make something not work well

   D make something clumsy

6. The word *predecessors* means

   F the dead

   G parents

   H ancestors

   J children

Using Context Clues

You know that clues in the surrounding sentence or paragraph can help you figure out the meaning of an unfamiliar word. Sometimes context can help you understand a word you simply don't know. And sometimes **context clues** can show you that a word you do know can have a different meaning.

Homographs are words that have the same spelling but different meanings. Sometimes they are pronounced differently. You need to depend on context clues to figure out which meaning is intended when you are reading. Listed below are some common homographs with their meanings.

affect to influence; to pretend
ball round object; formal dance
band group of musicians; a strip

baste to put liquid on while cooking; to sew with temporary stitches
minute sixty seconds; tiny
refrain to hold back; a repeated part

For each underlined word, write the meaning that fits the context of the sentence.

1. The nervous student <u>affected</u> an air of calm.

   _____

2. Some organizations sponsor a <u>ball</u> to raise money for charity.

   _____

3. Wrap large <u>bands</u> of rubber or other material around the package.

   _____

4. To cook a Thanksgiving turkey, <u>baste</u> it frequently with melted butter or oil.

   _____

5. The letters at the bottom of the page were too <u>minute</u> to be seen easily.

   _____

6. The chorus of a song is its <u>refrain</u>.

   _____

Practice

Context clues can help you choose which meaning is intended for each underlined word. Write the meaning on the line following the sentence.

1. **Despite** his appearance of strength, George Washington was often sick. (in contrast to; with bitter resentment)

   _____

2. Historians have **combed** through his diaries and letters. (groomed the hair; searched closely)

   _____

3. They have found **mention** of the illnesses he suffered. (a reference; speak about)

   _____

4. As a boy, he **nearly** died from diphtheria. (almost; closely)

   _____

5. Later in life he caught malaria, which would **plague** him for the rest of his life. (bother; rapidly spreading disease)

   _____

6. It is well known that Washington's teeth had to be **extracted**. (taken out; quoted)

   _____

7. As Washington neared the end of his second **term** as president, many people urged him to serve again. (a word with an exact meaning; a limited period of time)

   _____

8. He felt he had to **refuse** because of his health. (turn down; garbage)

   _____

9. So he **declined** to serve. (became worse; said no)

   _____

10. Washington is remembered as a strong leader in spite of his **poor** health. (not good; without money or resources)

   _____

Apply

Read the following paragraph. Use context clues to figure out the meaning of the underlined words. Then write the meaning on the line below.

All the woolly mammoths, ancient animals that looked like hairy elephants, died centuries ago, but some are still around. The Ice Age preserved some of the (creatures intact, that is, whole. In Siberia and Alaska, whole mammoths have been found frozen in ice. Some of these huge animals are as much as 25,000 years old. In some cases, the last meal the great beast ate is preserved in its stomach. Surprised scientists were amazed at the condition of the meat of the mammoth itself. The ice kept the animals in much the same way modern frozen food is preserved. When the mammoth meat was thawed, it was found to be tough but edible—though it was served only to dogs. Most of the earth's mammoths were probably killed off by humans before the Ice Age. Luckily, those that survived primitive hunters were frozen, making it possible for today's scientists to use them for research into the past.

1. woolly mammoths

_____

2. intact

_____

3. preserved

_____

4. amazed

_____

5. thawed

_____

6. edible

_____

7. primitive

_____

Check Up

Read the following passage. Then circle the answer for each question.

What follows you around all day, but almost vanishes at lunchtime? Well, it certainly isn't your dog or cat or your best friend—they would all like to have a bite of your noon repast. No, the constant companion that goes away only at noon is your shadow. For most of the morning, you cast a shadow by blocking the sun, which is low in the sky. The higher the sun rises, the smaller your shadow gets. That is because your body obstructs less light as the sun reaches its greatest height over your part of the earth. At noon, when the sun is directly overhead, you block almost no light. As a result, your shadow almost disappears.

1. The word *vanishes* means

   A leads

   B disappears

   C is conquered

   D is made shiny

2. The word *repast* means

   F what came before

   G thinking again about the past

   H a meal

   J recess

3. The word *constant* means

   A dark

   B terrible

   C favorite

   D unchanging

4. The word *cast* means

   F cause to fall

   G wrap in plaster

   H throw away

   J choose actors for a play

5. The word *blocking* means

   A laying out city blocks

   B getting in the way of

   C building with cubes

   D forgetting

6. The word *obstructs* means

   F builds

   G delays

   H gets in the way of

   J ruins

 **Read On**   Read "Dogs Who 'Think.'" As you read, watch for context clues to the meanings of new words. Then answer the questions.

Spelling Words

Spelling is an important writing skill. When you spell words correctly, your readers understand what you mean. Most English words are spelled with regular patterns. However, some words pose special difficulty.

Homonyms are words that sound alike or almost alike but are spelled differently. In order to spell the word correctly, you need to know which spelling goes with which meaning.

The meanings of common homonyms are listed below.

it's contraction for *it is*
its belonging to it

passed went beyond
past time gone by

their belonging to them
there in that place
they're contraction for *they are*

to toward
too also; very
two number after one; 2

who's contraction for *who is*
whose possessive form of *who*

your belonging to you
you're contraction for *you are*

Use one or both of the homonyms in parentheses to complete each sentence.

1. _____ backpack was left in the classroom? (Whose, Who's)

2. The boys say _____ coming back soon. (there, they're)

3. _____ time to paint the house; _____ color is faded. (it's, its)

4. Be sure _____ car is locked. (your, you're)

5. The bus _____ the correct exit and had to take the next one. (passed, past)

6. Sheila says she is _____ busy to go _____ the store. (to, too, two)

Practice

Homonyms are one kind of easily misspelled word. Experts who have studied people's writing have found that even good spellers often have trouble spelling certain other words.

Find five words that give you trouble in the following list of commonly misspelled words. Write each word, say it aloud to yourself, and then write a sentence that includes the word. Doing this should help you remember how to spell the word. Use a dictionary if you need to check definitions.

absence	conscience	height	receive	succeed
accommodate	conscious	license	recommend	surprise
achieve	embarrass	miscellaneous	reference	susceptible
although	enough	mysterious	referring	technique
apparent	exaggerate	occasion	repetition	through
arctic	exhausted	occurred	restaurant	tragedy
bargain	fascinate	parallel	rhythm	unnecessary
because	February	possession	seize	vacuum
believe	grammar	privilege	separate	vegetable
calendar	guarantee	procedure	straight	villain

1. word: _____

   sentence: _____

2. word: _____

   sentence: _____

3. word: _____

   sentence: _____

4. word: _____

   sentence: _____

5. word: _____

   sentence: _____

Apply

After you have written a first draft of a paper, you need to edit and proofread it before you can consider it final. **Proofreading** means to check for correct punctuation, capitalization, and spelling.

Look at the twelve underlined words. Find the six that are misspelled, and write them correctly on the lines below.

Their are snakes more dangerous than the cobra. Still, it would be wise not to fool around with one of these reptiles. The king cobra is by far the largest poisonous snake in the world. It can grow to a length of eighteen feat. Cobras live in India and southern China, among other places. When a cobra has a cents of danger, it emits an evil-sounding hiss. It lifts itself upright and expands its neck into a hood. On the back of its hood is a mark like a pear of spectacles. Then it sweeps forward to bite. Cobras are not so dangerous as generally believed because of the weigh they attack. A cobra's habit of sweeping to the attack, rather than darting forward quickly, makes it less of a threat than other snakes. Some cobras squirt poison at the eyes of the victim. This "spitting" is most developed in two African cobras and one East Indian cobra. Snake charmers pretend to charm cobras with music, but the snakes can here only a limited range of sounds and cannot hear music. When they look like they are being charmed, they are only holding themselves on guard. They would act the same way without music.

1. _____

2. _____

3. _____

4. _____

5. _____

6. _____

Check Up

For each sentence below, decide which of the spellings is correct to fill in the blank in the sentence. Then circle the answer.

1. Abraham Lincoln's birthday is in _____.

   A Febuary

   B Februery

   C February

   D Febrery

2. The city _____ meets twice a month.

   F counsel

   G council

   H concil

   J counsle

3. Mississippi is a _____ state.

   A southren

   B suthern

   C southern

   D sothern

4. Did you _____ the floor as well as dust?

   F vacuum

   G vaccum

   H vaccuum

   J vacume

5. People used to write letters on elegant _____.

   A stationary

   B stationery

   C statonary

   D stationry

6. Check for correct spelling and _____ as you revise your papers.

   F gramar

   G grammar

   H grammer

   J gramer

7. Do you know _____ gloves these are?

   A whos

   B who's

   C whoes

   D whose

8. I can _____ that restaurant.

   F reccommend

   G recommend

   H reccomend

   J recomend

More Spelling Words

A **suffix** is one or more syllables added to the end of a base word. Remember these spelling rules for adding suffixes:

- When adding a suffix beginning with a vowel to a word ending in a silent *e*, you usually drop the *e*. (fame + -ous = famous)
- When adding a suffix beginning with a consonant to a word ending in silent *e*, you usually keep the *e*. (care + -ful = careful)
- When adding a suffix to a word ending in *y* preceded by a consonant, change the *y* to *i*. (pretty + -est = prettiest; silly + -ness = silliness)
- When adding *-ing, -ed,* or *-er* to words of one syllable that end in a consonant preceded by a vowel, double the final consonant. (shop + -ing = shopping)

Complete each sentence by combining the suffix and the word in parentheses. Write the word in the blank. Use a dictionary if necessary.

1. (-er, windy) Today is much _____ than yesterday.

2. (-ive, relate) My great uncle is one _____ I had not met before the family reunion.

3. (-age, store) Those new apartments have very little _____

4. (-ant, triumph) The school's athletes felt _____ after they won the meet.

5. (-or, translate) Because the woman spoke seven languages, she easily found work

   as a _____ in an international company.

6. (-er, destroy) The _____ was sunk by a torpedo.

7. (-ing, stir) Keep _____ the soup or it will burn.

8. (-able, compare) The cheaper shoes are not _____ in quality to the more expensive ones.

9. (-ment, arrange) The florist provided an _____ of spring flowers for the centerpiece.

10. (-ful, beauty) The woods are _____ in the fall.

Practice

Find the misspelled word in each of the following sentences. Then write the word correctly. Use a dictionary if necessary.

1. George Pullman had an idea that profounddly changed the face of travel forever.

   _____

2. His dream was to bring luxuryous train travel to the masses.

   _____

3. In April of 1865, the Pullman sleepping car made its initial run.

   _____

4. With its elegant woodwork, spring beds, and plush carpets, the car was like a moveing hotel.

   _____

5. However, the car's width stoped it from crossing many railroad bridges.

   _____

6. The railroads soon found themselves replaceing the narrower bridges with wider ones.

   _____

7. Pullman was happy with his succesful sleeper.

   _____

8. Unfortunatly, that first run in 1865 was a somber one.

   _____

9. That day the new car carryed the body of Abraham Lincoln.

   _____

10. The first Pullman served as a hearse for the late president who was being taken back to Illinois for buryal.

    _____

Apply

Proofread the following paragraphs for spelling errors. Find eight misspelled words, and write them correctly on the lines below.

It's dark. The camppers have made it through the day safly. The camp canoes are tied to their moorrings. The last of the hamburgers and hot dogs have been eaten. A knot of satisfyed campers and camp counselors is sitting around an open fire. Someone shouts, "Who's for roastting marshmallows?"

"Great idea," shouts another.

"Why are they called marshmallows?" wonders a kid next to the head counsellor.

The bearded counselor says, "The marshmallows we're roasting are made from proceced corn syrup. Obvioussly, they don't grow in marshes. But at one time, back in England, there was a candy made from a relative of the cotton plant called the marshmallow. The white marshmallows I'm holding look a lot like the seedpods of the marshmallow plant. And that is how the marshmallow got its name."

1. _____

2. _____

3. _____

4. _____

5. _____

6. _____

7. _____

8. _____

Check Up

For each sentence below, decide which of the spellings is correct to fill in the blank in the sentence. Then circle the answer.

1. The mayor hosted a _____ after the dedication of the new city hall.

   A reception

   B recepshion

   C receivetion

   D reseption

2. August was the _____ month of the year.

   F hotiest

   G hottest

   H hotest

   J hottiest

3. His sense of _____ helped him through trying times.

   A determineation

   B determination

   C determinned

   D determineing

4. The children _____ rope during recess.

   F jumpped

   G jumpy

   H jumped

   J jumpping

5. There were seven members on the _____ committee.

   A adviseary

   B adviseory

   C adviceory

   D advisory

6. That is the _____ hat I have ever seen!

   F ugliest

   G uglyest

   H uglyiest

   J uglest

7. The doctor wrote a _____ for new medicine.

   A presription

   B prescripton

   C prescription

   D perscription

8. The maintenance man was _____ for all building repairs.

   F responsible

   G responsable

   H responseble

   J responseable

Read On   Read "Dark Days." Answer the questions and consider the spelling of words.

Review

Synonyms

Words that have about the same meanings are called **synonyms**.

A lion is a natural <u>foe</u> of a zebra, so zebras fear lions.

A *foe* is an enemy.

Antonyms

Words with opposite meanings are called **antonyms**.

After the storm hit, the mayor <u>calmly</u> took charge.

An antonym for *calmly* is *peacefully*.

Context Clues

You can figure out the meaning of a word by using clues from the words, phrases, and sentences around it.

Tim had a <u>receipt</u> to prove that he had paid for his purchase.

A *receipt* is a note showing payment has been made.

Spelling Words

Words that sound alike but are spelled differently are **homonyms**.

The <u>bare</u> trees signaled that winter was near. (not <u>bear</u> trees)

A **suffix** is a word part added to the end of a base word. Sometimes the spelling of a base word changes when a suffix is added.

The puppy looked <u>pitiful</u> as it sat in the rain.

Assessment

Circle the answer that is a synonym for each underlined word.

1. many <u>parts</u> of a puzzle

   A pegs

   B pieces

   C colors

   D kinds

2. modern urban <u>structure</u>

   F building

   G desk

   H fountain

   J highway

3. <u>precious</u> gem

   A much loved

   B pretty

   C valuable

   D shiny

4. good <u>suggestion</u>

   F idea

   G question

   H problem

   J sentence

Circle the answer that is an antonym for each underlined word.

5. <u>innocent</u> person

   A guilty

   B moral

   C sly

   D honest

6. <u>rural</u> area

   F country

   G urban

   H crowded

   J popular

7. <u>include</u> your friends

   A explore

   B invite

   C announce

   D exclude

8. <u>casual</u> clothes

   F loose

   G clean

   H formal

   J expensive

Circle each correct spelling.

9. sack of _____

   A flower

   B floure

   C flour

   D flowr

10. _____ bouquet of roses

    F beauttiful

    G beautyful

    H beautyfull

    J beautiful

Read each paragraph and circle the answer for each question.

Newts belong to the same family as frogs and toads. Newts are amphibians. They spend part of their time in water and part out. Two kinds of newts live in the United States. The red-spotted newt is native to the East. The Pacific newt is native to the West. Each strain eats insects, tadpoles, worms, and small fish.

11. The word *amphibian* means

   A animals that live in water only

   B animals that live on land only

   C animals that live in water and on land

   D animals that live in the East and West

12. In this paragraph *strain* means

   F to filter something

   G a great effort

   H to squeeze out

   J a type or kind

If you have ever gotten a blister, you probably don't want to get another one. Unfortunately, the chances are pretty good that you will. These annoying little sores can appear in seconds and sometimes take days to heal. If you play sports, even the littlest blister can affect the way you play. Friction is the main cause of blisters, and more often than not, people get them on their feet. You can avoid blisters by wearing shoes that fit well—that are neither too big nor too small. This decreases the chance that your shoes will rub against parts of your feet.

13. In this paragraph, *blister* means

   A a bubblelike projection used for observation in an aircraft or train

   B a transparent package for merchandise

   C a raised patch of skin caused by rubbing

   D a harsh argument

14. Something that is *annoying* is

   F painful

   G easily formed

   H bothersome

   J itchy

An HMO is a group medical plan. A group of doctors provide care for people who <u>subscribe</u> to the plan. In most HMOs, patients pay a <u>flat fee</u> each month. This way, they pay for medical care a little bit at a time.

15. The word *subscribe* means

    A to agree to receive and pay for

    B to ask a doctor questions

    C to request surgery

    D to get a magazine

16. A *flat fee* is

    F stale and tasteless

    G smooth and level

    H without money

    J fixed and unchanging

Everyone knows that snails are slowpokes. But exactly how slow are they? The snail is the slowest-crawling creature on Earth. Some varieties can crawl as much as 150 feet in an hour. But they're the real speedsters of the snail family. The ordinary land sail can't travel anywhere near that fast. The fastest land snail ever <u>clocked</u> moved just two feet in the space of three minutes. That is equivalent to 40 feet, or seven-thousandths of a mile, per hour. So, to stroll just one mile would take the faster land snail five and a half days.

17. Snails do seem to get where they're going eventually, but the going is pretty

    A fast

    B slow

    C uneven

    D crooked

18. In this paragraph, a good synonym for *clocked* would be

    F watched

    G pushed

    H timed

    J raced

What's Cooking?

When you follow a recipe, you need to pay close attention to details and sequence. Read the recipe and answer the questions.

Tex-Mex Pizzas

Ingredients
1 16-oz. can pinto beans
6 flour tortillas, 10-inch size
6 tsp. olive oil
1 cup salsa
6 green onions, chopped
1 zucchini, thinly sliced
1 yellow squash, thinly sliced
1 cup black olives, chopped
1 cup low-fat cheese, shredded
Yield: 6 servings
Pan: Large baking sheets
Temperature: Broil

Directions:
1. Preheat the broiler.
2. Drain and mash the pinto beans. Set aside.

3. Brush one side of each tortilla with 1 teaspoon oil. Place on baking sheet oil-side down.
4. Combine mashed pinto beans and salsa in bowl.
5. Spread one-sixth of the bean mixture on each tortilla.
6. Sprinkle evenly with green onions, zucchini, yellow squash, olives, and cheese.
7. Place baking sheet under the broiler on rack.
8. Broil 8 to 10 minutes. Watch carefully so tortillas do not burn.
9. Serve hot.

---

1. At what temperature do you set the oven? _____

2. What is the first thing you do to the tortillas? _____

3. What do you do to the pinto beans before spreading them on the tortillas?

   _____

4. Which ingredient uses 6 teaspoons? _____

5. How many servings does this recipe make? _____

Abbreviations

Writers often use shortened forms of words, or abbreviations. Write the letter of the correct word next to the abbreviation.

1. gal	_____	**A**	foot
2. ave.	_____	**B**	year
3. blvd.	_____	**C**	quart
4. lb	_____	**D**	avenue
5. ft	_____	**E**	time from noon to midnight
6. hr	_____	**F**	inch
7. yr.	_____	**G**	pound
8. NY	_____	**H**	January
9. P.M.	_____	**I**	United States
10. Dec.	_____	**J**	Wisconsin
11. NV	_____	**K**	gallon
12. qt	_____	**L**	hour
13. Mr.	_____	**M**	General
14. in.	_____	**N**	yard
15. Jan.	_____	**O**	Mister
16. U.S.	_____	**P**	Doctor
17. yd	_____	**Q**	boulevard
18. WI	_____	**R**	Nevada
19. Dr.	_____	**S**	December
20. Gen.	_____	**T**	New York

Recognizing Details

Paragraphs are often made up mostly of **details** that support a **main idea**. The main idea is the most important point the writer wants to make. If the main idea is not stated, you can determine what it is from the details.

Poison in many plants keeps animals from eating them. The leaves and the nectar of mountain laurel are poisonous when eaten. Some plants protect themselves by being poisonous to the touch. The tissues of poison ivy contain an oil that is irritating to the skin. The bristles of a nettle are poisonous. Animals can get a rash from touching them. Animals that try to eat poisonous plants soon learn to look elsewhere for food.

The main idea of this paragraph is: *Plants protect themselves from being eaten by animals in several ways.*

These details support the main idea: *The leaves and the nectar of mountain laurel are poisonous when eaten. The tissues of poison ivy contain an oil that is irritating to the skin. The bristles of a nettle are poisonous. Animals can get a rash from touching them.*

Read the paragraph. Then answer the questions.

You don't see many pots and pans with metal handles. There's a good reason. Metal gets hot very quickly. If you leave a metal spoon in a hot bowl of soup, the spoon will get as hot as the soup. A metal handle on a pan also gets hot. Metal is a good material for a frying pan. It gets hot and stays hot. But the heat from the stove heats the metal handle, too. That's why pan handles should not be made of metal.

1. What is the main idea of this paragraph?

   _____

2. What details support the main idea?

   _____

   _____

Practice

Read each paragraph. Then circle the answer for each question.

Glass snakes are fragile. They are a kind of legless lizard that has a breakable tail. Glass snakes live in the United States and Mexico. They grow to be about two feet long. Their tails are usually twice as long as their bodies. Glass snakes use their tails to distract their enemies. When it is being chased, a glass snake breaks off its tail. The tail then starts to twitch while the glass snake gets away. The enemy attacks the twitching tail instead of the glass snake. Glass snakes then grow new tails.

1. Which sentence states the main idea of this paragraph?

   A Glass snakes are a type of legless lizard.

   B Some lizards have interesting ways to protect themselves.

   C Glass snakes are able to grow new body parts.

   D Glass snakes live in warm climates.

2. Which detail does **not** support the main idea of this paragraph?

   F When it is being chased, a glass snake breaks off its tail.

   G The enemy attacks the twitching tail instead of the glass snake.

   H The tail then starts to twitch while the glass snake gets away.

   J Their tails are usually twice as long as their bodies.

Many people who live near or visit the seashore collect seashells. I like to visit the beach in the morning. Some people collect shells with the sea creatures still in them. These shells are likely to be in the best shape. Others just collect empty shells from the beach. The best time to find empty shells is when they've washed up on the beach after a storm. Collectors can clean and label shells. Some people make jewelry and decorations out of the prettiest shells.

3. Which sentence states the main idea of this paragraph?

   A Most shells can be found on beaches after storms.

   B Many people enjoy collecting seashells.

   C Bracelets and earrings can be made from seashells.

   D People enjoy hobbies.

4. Which detail does **not** support the main idea of this paragraph?

   F Some people collect shells with the sea creatures still in them.

   G Collectors can clean and label shells.

   H Others just collect empty shells from the beach.

   J I like to visit the beach in the morning.

Apply

Read each paragraph. Then circle the answer that completes each statement.

Molds can be found in many places. Some sprout in jars or on leftover food. Some grow on their own, often when and where you don't want them to. Molds are like mushrooms and mildew. They are members of the fungus family. Most molds look like fuzz. They feed on the sugar that is in bread, fruit, and other foods. Mold will often spoil a food's taste. Although moldy food should usually be thrown away, certain cheeses owe their flavors to the mold that grows in them and ripens them.

1. According to the passage, all molds

   A are mushrooms

   B are always harmful

   C look like fuzz

   D are a kind of fungus

2. Molds grow on

   F leftover food

   G jars

   H fuzz

   J mildew

Have you ever wondered where all the salt in the ocean came from? If you have, then you are not alone. Scientists have been trying to figure this out as well. No one knows the answer for sure. Even scientists can only make a good guess. Here is one theory about sea salt. Long ago Earth was dry. Many of the rocks on Earth contained salt. The oceans were formed by heavy rains that fell for a long time. The rains washed salt off the rocks and into the oceans as they were being made. After a time, the oceans were full of salt. Today there is about a quarter of a pound of salt in every gallon of sea water.

3. According to one theory, sea salt came from

   A rain

   B rocks

   C mines

   D oceans

4. How much salt is there in sea water today?

   F No one knows.

   G a quarter of a pound per gallon

   H a pound per gallon

   J a gallon

Check Up

Read the paragraph. Then circle the answer that best completes each statement.

Large rocks were used to build some churches in the Middle Ages. They were often brought from as much as 50 miles away. Workers on foot carried each stone from the quarry to the building site. No one person ever carried a rock the whole 50 miles, though. Instead, a relay system, much like a "bucket brigade" for fighting fires, was used. In a bucket brigade, the people of a town would stand in a line. They would stand between the burning building and a nearby pond. They passed buckets of water hand to hand, from the pond to the fire. The same system was used for moving heavy stones to the building sites of the churches.

1. Often a title states the main idea. What is the best title for this paragraph?

   A Building Gothic Churches

   B The "Stone Brigade"

   C The "Bucket Brigade"

   D Quarrying Stones

2. What were bucket brigades organized to do?

   F put out fires

   G carry drinking water

   H carry large stones

   J build churches

3. Large rocks were brought to the construction site of churches by

   A a system of levers

   B people carrying them in a relay system

   C people in carts

   D a single person carrying a rock 50 miles

4. A relay system is a method for

   F running a race

   G passing something from one person to the next

   H building churches

   J gathering rocks

Recalling Details

Details are facts that support the main idea of a passage. When you read, it is important to recognize the main idea and its supporting details. Sometimes deciding which details are important depends on your purpose for reading.

Read the paragraph. Then answer the questions.

A strange kind of rain sometimes falls over northern Australia. Tornadoes sometimes occur with thunderstorms. Together they cause strong whirlwinds to form above the sea. These winds are so strong that they can lift water, seaweed, and driftwood. They can even lift whole schools of fish from the water! Sometimes hundreds of fish are carried inland by the storms. The fish finally fall from the sky. They land in fields and on roofs. In this part of the world, instead of raining cats and dogs, it sometimes rains fish!

1. What is the main idea of this paragraph?

   _____

   _____

   _____

2. Write three details that support the main idea.

   _____

   _____

   _____

Practice

A reading passage often has several paragraphs. Each paragraph will have its own main idea. Each paragraph will be about the topic. The main ideas of all the paragraphs are supporting details for the whole topic.

Read the passage. Then answer the questions.

All the clothes that cowhands wear serve a purpose. Some parts seem to be just decoration. But each item helps protect the cowhand on the range.

Boots have pointed toes and high heels. The pointed toes slip easily into the stirrups on a saddle. The heels keep the boots from sliding through the stirrups and throwing the cowhand off-balance. Cowhands wear tall boots to protect their legs from snakes and sharp branches.

Hats have wide brims to shade the cowhand's face and neck. A bandanna, or neckerchief, absorbs sweat. When the wind raises dust, the cowhand reties the cloth around the nose and mouth to keep out the dust.

1. The title can tell the main idea of an article. What would be a good title for this article?

   _____

   _____

2. What are two important details that support the selection's main idea?

   _____

   _____

3. Think about the details the writer has used in this passage. Where might you read a passage like this?

   _____

   _____

Apply

Read each paragraph. Then answer the questions.

Many people struck it rich during the gold rush in the Klondike. In 1898 the town of Dawson was filled with prospectors. Thousands of people went to Dawson hoping to make their fortunes. A few of them did without mining for gold. The prospectors had to eat. Some sly business people set up grocery stores in Dawson. The prospectors had no choice but to buy from them. Dawson grocers sold milk for sixteen dollars a gallon. They sold eggs for three dollars a dozen. The many people who went seeking gold were taking a risk. Those who set up stores and sold groceries to the miners were certain of making their fortunes.

Write two details from the passage about the Klondike gold rush.

1. _____

2. _____

Write two details from the passage about the prices in grocery stores in Dawson.

3. _____

4. _____

5. What is the main idea that these details support?

_____

Most creatures with backbones also have tails. But not all creatures use their tails for the same purpose. Some use their tails as an extra arm. Monkeys use their tails to swing from branch to branch. Cows use their tails as built-in fly swatters. They swish their tails back and forth to keep insects away. The tail on a fish helps it swim. Foxes use their bushy tails to cover their paws and noses at night to keep them warm.

Write three details from the passage about how animals use their tails.

6. _____

_____

_____

Check Up

Read the passage below. Then circle the answer for each question.

Children have been singing about "cockles and mussels" for many years. But many people don't know what they are. Both are types of shellfish. Mussels are the better known of the two. Freshwater mussels are common in North American lakes. They look like skinny, deep blue clams.

Cockles are rarely found along American shores. They are similar to soft-shelled clams. The coast of Wales is covered with cockles. One 320-acre area was estimated to hold 450 million cockles. In Wales, the cockle-pickers are always busy. Whole villages depend on cockle-gathering to make a living. Cockles reproduce and grow very rapidly. The frequent digging does very little to slow them down. A whole bed of cockles, however, may suddenly decide to move to a new place. When this happens, the people who pick cockles have to pack up and move, too.

1. What is the best title for this selection?

   A Cockles in Wales

   B Old Children's Songs

   C Two Kinds of Shellfish

   D Mussels in North American Lakes

2. Suppose you were going to write a research paper in which you describe cockles. Which one of these details would be important to you?

   F Cockles are rarely found along American shores.

   G They look like skinny, deep blue clams.

   H They are similar to soft-shell clams.

   J In Wales, the cockle-pickers are always busy.

3. What are two important supporting details of this selection?

   A Mussels look like skinny, deep blue clams. A bed of mussels can relocate itself.

   B People who pick mussels in Wales are always busy. Cockles reproduce and grow rapidly.

   C Mussels are common in North America. Cockles are common in Wales.

   D Cockles and mussels are mentioned in a children's song. Many people know a great deal about cockles and mussels.

4. What happens when a whole bed of cockles moves to a new place?

   F Villagers bring them back.

   G The cockle-pickers are kept busy.

   H The people who pick from that bed follow it.

   J The cockles reproduce quickly.

Read On   Look for details as you read "Diamonds: Stars from Earth." Then answer the questions.

Recognizing Sequence

The order in which events take place is called **sequence**. It is important to know what happens first, second, and so on. Look for clue words such as *first, next, then,* and *last.*

Read the paragraph. Then circle the answer for each question.

Wood is the major source of paper-making fibers in the United States. First, trees are cut into logs and transported to a mill. Next, the wood is washed. It is cut into small chips. Then it is treated with chemicals to release the fibers. The fibers are mixed with fillings and dyes into a smooth pulp. Then the wood pulp passes through screens to remove unwanted materials. After the pulp has drained on a wire mesh, suction devices remove remaining water. Stacks of rollers smooth the surface of the paper. The paper is wound on giant reels. Finally, it is shipped to factories to be made into finished products.

1. What is the first step in the paper-making process after wood arrives at a paper mill?

    A washing the wood

    B cutting the wood into small chips

    C cutting down trees

    D passing the pulp through screens

2. When are dyes added?

    F after the fibers have been treated with chemicals

    G after the water has been removed from the pulp

    H after the paper is wound on reels

    J before the logs are transported to the mill

3. When do suction devices remove the remaining water?

    A before the fillings and dyes are added

    B after rollers smooth the paper

    C after it is shipped to factories

    D after the pulp has been drained on a wire mesh

4. Reread the paragraph. List the words that were clues to the order of steps in making paper.

    _____

    _____

    _____

    _____

Practice

Read the passage. Then circle the answer for each question.

The world lost a great pilot when Amelia Earhart's plane vanished in 1937. Earhart was making a trip around the world when her plane went down in the Pacific Ocean. A navy ship picked up a radio message from Earhart. She said she had no fuel. Searchers could not find a trace of her plane. Earhart had been a nurse during World War I. Then she moved to California to take flying lessons. Soon she bought her own plane. She set a flying record for women. She was the first female passenger to cross the Atlantic Ocean by air. Later she became the first woman pilot to fly across the Atlantic Ocean.

1. Which of these events happened first in Amelia Earhart's life?

   A Amelia Earhart was a nurse in World War I.

   B Amelia Earhart flew across the Atlantic Ocean alone.

   C Amelia Earhart took flying lessons.

   D Amelia Emhart sent a message to a navy ship.

2. When did Amelia Earhart buy her own plane?

   F before World War I

   G after 1937

   H before she moved to California

   J after she moved to California

3. What happened in 1937?

   A Earhart set a flying record for women.

   B Earhart's plane vanished.

   C Earhart took flying lessons.

   D Earhart became the first woman passenger to cross the Atlantic Ocean.

4. Which event from Amelia Earhart's life took place last?

   F Earhart bought an airplane.

   G Earhart sent a radio message from somewhere in the Pacific.

   H Earhart set a flying record for women.

   J Earhart flew across the Atlantic Ocean.

Apply

Read each paragraph. Then write the steps in the order that they happen.

Wasps build nests that are a lot like beehives. But wasps don't make honey. They raise young wasps in their nests. Wasp nests have many sections. First, they separate the sections with bits of grass, stone, or mud. Then the queen lays one egg in each section. The worker wasps take care of the eggs. They feed the baby wasps after they hatch. Finally, the young wasps grow up and learn to fly.

Steps: The Life Cycle of a Wasp

1. _____

2. _____

3. _____

4. _____

5. _____

Have you ever wondered what the patent office does? The patent office keeps track of new products and their inventors. The first thing an inventor should do is record the date the invention came to mind. Next, he or she should draw a sketch with a description of the idea. Then two witnesses should sign the document. The inventor pays a filing fee when he or she submits an application. After the form is filed, the patent office checks to make sure that no one else has a patent for the same thing. If the application is accepted, the patent office gives the invention a patent number. This gives the inventor the legal right to the idea for 20 years.

Steps: Obtaining a Patent

1. _____

2. _____

3. _____

4. _____

5. _____

6. _____

Check Up

Read the passage. Then circle the answer for each question.

The fiddler crab changes the color of its shell over the course of each day. It is light at night and dark during the day. It is darkest at noon. Then the fiddler crab lightens as night falls. The color change may be the fiddler crab's camouflage. The fiddler crab adapts its color change to changes in the length of the day. In the winter, when night falls earlier, the fiddler crab gets lighter earlier each evening.

Some scientists wondered what would happen to the fiddler crab in a place where there were no day or night. They put the crab in a laboratory home. They kept the light at a constant level. The crab changed color just as it had on its home beach. It seems that the fiddler crab has a built-in clock that signals the color change. The fiddler crab's built-in clock can be reset. When the scientists moved fiddler crabs to a beach in a different time zone, the crabs changed color according to their new day.

1. When is the fiddler crab's shell light?

    A when it is in a laboratory

    B when it is light outside

    C when it is dark outside

    D after its biological clock is reset

2. When is the fiddler crab's shell darkest?

    F at noon

    G at dawn

    H at night

    J when it is in the laboratory

3. What happens before the crab's shell changes color earlier each evening?

    A spring begins

    B summer begins

    C the days get longer

    D the days get shorter

4. What did the scientists do before they put crabs in the laboratory?

    F They moved the crabs to a different time zone.

    G They decided the crabs had a built-in clock.

    H They wondered what would happen with no day or night.

    J They kept the light at a constant level.

Understanding Sequence

A **sequence of events** follows a certain time order. In stories and articles, however, writers do not always present the events in the order in which they happen.

Read the passage. Number the events in the order in which they occur.

In the 1700s, a French fisherman made a catch that was worth more than all the fish he could catch in ten years. As he pulled in his nets, he noticed a large object shaped like a plate. It was covered with mud. The fisherman thought it was useless. He sold it to a silversmith who found it interesting. The silversmith took it home and polished it. He discovered that it was pure silver. It was perfectly round. It measured over two feet in diameter. He wanted to sell it. He divided it into four pieces. A wealthy merchant bought one piece. The merchant was fascinated with it. He bought the other three pieces as well. He had the pieces rejoined. He carefully looked at the object. He saw it that it was a shield from a powerful family of ancient France.

1. _____ The silversmith polished the object.

2. _____ The fisherman sold his catch to a silversmith.

3. _____ The pieces were rejoined.

4. _____ The silversmith divided the object into four pieces.

5. _____ A fisherman made a special catch.

6. _____ The merchant identified the plate as the shield of a powerful family.

7. _____ The silversmith found out that the object was silver.

8. _____ He liked the piece so much that he bought the other three pieces.

9. _____ A merchant bought the first piece.

10. _____ The merchant carefully examined the plate.

Practice

Read the paragraph and think about the sequence of events. Then answer the questions.

      The movers loaded the last of the furniture into the van. Ana turned and looked at her house one last time. She remembered the fun times she had had there. She thought about the time she and her best friend Lee set up a fruit stand in the front yard. They had spent two days picking apples and making signs. Then they delivered flyers to everyone in the neighborhood. It was a beautiful fall day. The girls set the fruit on a table in the yard. The apples looked good enough to eat. And that's just what Ana and Lee did. They ate all of the apples before the first shopper stopped at the fruit stand. Ana sighed. Just then Lee crossed the street to say good-bye.

1. Which happened first in Ana's life, the movers loaded the truck or Ana and Lee picked the apples?

   _____

   _____

2. When did Ana and Lee deliver the flyers to their neighbors—right after they picked the apples or just before Lee said good-bye?

   _____

   _____

3. On the day of the apple sale, what did Ana and Lee do first?

   _____

   _____

4. Did Ana and Lee sell any apples? How do you know?

   _____

   _____

5. What happens last in this story?

   _____

   _____

Apply

Read the paragraph and think about the sequence of events. Then answer the questions.

In colonial times, making maple syrup was a long process. In the late winter or early spring, the farmer made a small hole in each maple tree trunk and put a spout in the hole. He hung a wooden bucket from each spout. When the buckets were full of sap, he emptied them into storage barrels. The sap was then boiled in huge kettles. When enough water had been boiled away, the sap became syrup. Then the syrup was passed through a flannel strainer to remove any impurities. Some syrup was boiled longer until maple sugar formed.

1. What did the farmer have to do before hanging a bucket from a maple tree?

_____

_____

2. At what time of year did the maple sugaring take place?

_____

_____

3. What happened to the buckets after they filled with syrup?

_____

_____

4. At what point in the process did the sap become syrup?

_____

_____

5. What was done to the syrup right before it was boiled to became maple sugar?

_____

_____

Check Up

Read the paragraph. Then circle the answer for each question.

The world's first stamp collector began collecting just a year after the world's first postage stamp was introduced. Stamps were first issued in Great Britain in 1840. Before that, people had to take all their mail to the post office to pay for postage. Then Sir Rowland Hill had the idea of issuing stamps. With stamps bought in advance, people did not have to go to the post office. They could simply drop their stamped mail in the nearest mailbox. But soon a young woman dreamed up another use for stamps. She ran an ad in *The London Times* asking for canceled stamps. She wanted to wallpaper her room with them. She used the stamps for an unusual purpose. This woman was the world's first stamp collector.

1. When did the woman run the ad in *The London Times?*

   A 1840

   B 1841

   C 1842

   D 1843

2. Which one of the following events happened before Sir Rowland Hill had the idea of issuing stamps?

   F A woman became the first stamp collector.

   G People took all their mail to the post office.

   H People dropped their mail in the nearest mailbox.

   J A woman placed an ad in *The London Times.*

3. Which of the following events happened first?

   A A woman wallpapered her room with stamps.

   B A woman ran the ad in *The London Times.*

   C Stamps were first issued.

   D Sir Roland Hill had the idea of issuing stamps.

4. Which of the following events happened last?

   F The world's first postage stamp was introduced.

   G A woman ran an ad in *The London Times.*

   H The woman wallpapered her room with stamps.

   J People could buy stamps in advance.

Read On   As you read "The Courage of Harry Wu," look for the sequence of events. Then answer the questions.

Recognizing Stated Concepts

In factual material, an author states facts and ideas, or concepts. When you read factual material, look for these **stated concepts.** They provide information about topics.

Read the paragraph. Then write the answers.

The gas in your stove has probably traveled a long distance. Most natural gas is trapped below the earth's surface. Shafts are drilled through the ground to get this gas. Then the gas is pumped through huge pipelines. Some pipes are 42 inches in diameter. The gas is pumped at high pressure. A network of pipes covers the country. The gas arrives in pipes at the gas company. From there it is sent out to homes through more pipes. Someone who lives in New York might be getting gas that has come all the way from Texas. That's a trip of more than 1,500 miles!

1. Write the sentence that states the most important concept of the paragraph—the one that sums up what the whole paragraph is about.

   _____

   _____

2. Which is the more important concept to remember—that the gas is pumped through huge pipelines or that the pipes are 42 inches in diameter? Explain your answer.

   _____

   _____

3. Use your own words to explain where natural gas comes from before it gets to your stove.

   _____

   _____

   _____

   _____

Practice

Read each paragraph. Write *stated* or *not stated* after each sentence that follows. Note that something may be stated in different words.

Imagine attending Harvard College in the 17th century. Only male students were allowed to attend. Every boy who wished to enter the school had to know Latin. He had to be able to read, write, and speak the ancient language. The school was small and not very rich. There was only one fireplace to heat the whole college. The school's few students studied together in a large room where they had only candles to see by.

1. Harvard College was founded in 1636. _____

2. Students at Harvard in the 17th century had to study by candlelight. _____

3. Students could study together in one large room. _____

Many people think that Mt. Everest is the tallest mountain in the world. Well, they're wrong. There is one even taller. It is called Mauna Kea. Mauna Kea is the tallest mountain on Earth. It is 33,476 feet high. Mt. Everest is only 29,028 feet high. Many climbers have tackled Mt. Everest. Climbing Mauna Kea would not be practical. Most of Mauna Kea is under the Pacific Ocean. Only the top part of the mountain is above water. Actually, people go here all the time—the top part of Mauna Kea is the island called Hawaii.

4. Comparing the heights of mountains is not as simple as it might seem.

_____

5. The top part of Mauna Kea is the island of Hawaii. _____

6. Mauna Kea looks smaller than Mt. Everest because it is mostly under water.

_____

Apply

Read the paragraphs. Then answer the questions.

Most people know that there are craters on the moon. They can see the craters with a small telescope. A crater is a huge hole that is created when a large rock from space crashes into the surface of a planet or moon. The moon is covered with craters. Earth has very few. Earth's atmosphere causes many rocks from space to burn up before they reach the surface. But a few rocks survive and make craters on Earth. People in Arizona have proof of this. They live in the state that is the home of the Meteor Crater, the largest crater on Earth.

1. Why does Earth have fewer craters than the moon?

   _____

   Is that concept stated or not stated? _____

2. Where is the largest crater on Earth?

   _____

   Is that concept stated or not stated? _____

The brain is the center of the nervous system. All of your nerves are connected to your brain. When you feel something, your nerves are sending a message to your brain. But the brain itself has no nerves. It is well protected by the skull. It has no need for nerves to keep it from getting hurt. This lack of nerves has made some types of brain surgery possible. Surgeons can do some brain surgeries without anesthetics or pain-killers.

3. What part of the body is the center of the nervous system?

   _____

   Is that concept stated or not stated? _____

4. Does your brain feel pain?

   _____

   Is that concept stated or not stated? _____

Check Up

Read the paragraphs. Then circle the answer for each question.

Some of the creatures that live in the ocean cannot breathe underwater. Like many land animals, they are mammals. Mammals are animals that give birth to live babies instead of laying eggs. Mammals also grow hair and breathe air. Sea mammals don't get oxygen from water as fish do. Sea mammals have well-developed lungs. They can hold their breath for a long time. Whales, porpoises, and dolphins are all sea mammals. They don't dive and surface just for fun. They have to come out of the water to breathe.

1. Which of the following concepts was stated?

   A People are mammals.

   B Otters and seals are sea mammals.

   C Mammals cannot breathe underwater.

   D People enjoy watching dolphins.

2. What major difference between fish and whales was stated in this paragraph?

   F Fish get oxygen from the water but whales cannot.

   G Whales are much bigger than any fish.

   H Whales like to play on the surface of the water but fish do not.

   J Whales stay in deep water, but some fish can be found in shallow water.

Are you left-handed? If so, you use your left hand more than your right hand. Left-handed people use their left hands to do what many people do with their right hands. This causes left handers problems in our right-handed world. Scissors, for example, are made to fit into the right hand. Left-handed people have a hard time cutting things. When left-handed people sit in some classroom chairs, they find that the book rest is on the right side. Then they have to lean over to write.

3. Which of the following concepts was stated?

   A Most tools are designed for use by right-handed people.

   B Left-handed people use their left hands more than their right hands.

   C Only 3 percent of people are left-handed.

   D Some people are born with conditions that give them special problems.

4. Which of the following concepts was **not** stated?

   F Left-handed people often learn to use tools designed for right-handed people.

   G Most scissors are made for right-handed people.

   H When left-handed people sit in some classroom chairs, they have to lean over to write.

   J Left-handed people have a hard time cutting things.

Recalling Stated Concepts

Stated concepts usually provide the most important points in an article. Remember or note these concepts for later use.

Read the paragraph. Then circle the answer for each question.

Hummingbirds are very good fliers. These tiny birds may be the sky's most skillful pilots. Flying backwards is one trick that they perform easily. Most other birds must land or fly to a higher level gradually, but not the hummingbird! It can drop straight down or fly straight up. And of all the birds in nature, only the hummingbird can hover in midair. That is why this bird is often compared to a helicopter. The hummingbird has a strong set of wings. Its wings beat so quickly that they make a whirring noise. This is what gives the bird the hum for which it is named.

1. Which is **not** mentioned as something a hummingbird can do?

   A fly backwards

   B fly straight up

   C hover in midair

   D fly sideways

2. What is a hummingbird compared to in this passage?

   F an airplane

   G a helicopter

   H a rocket

   J a parachute

3. According to the paragraph, in what way is a hummingbird different from other birds?

   A It can hover in midair.

   B It cannot move around on land.

   C It cannot swim.

   D It beats its wings 70 times a second.

4. What is a hummingbird named after?

   F the whirring noise its wings make

   G the song it sings when it flies

   H the shape of its wings

   J the noise a helicopter makes

Practice

Read each paragraph. Then circle the answer for each question.

A bolt of lightning is a great spark caused by an electrical current. Water droplets in thunderclouds are charged with electricity. Some clouds have a positive charge. Others have a negative charge. Opposite charges attract each other. When they meet, they form a lightning bolt. Lightning can also take place within one cloud or between a cloud and the earth. A bolt of lightning can kill a person or start a fire.

1. Why is lightning so dangerous?

   A It can kill a person or start a fire.

   B It causes thunder.

   C It can strike tall buildings.

   D It signals that bad weather is approaching.

2. What is lightning?

   F a water droplet charged with electricity

   G a great spark caused by an electrical current

   H a light made from dust particles

   J a column of fast-moving air

You have tears in your eyes all the time. They are even there when you aren't crying. Eyes need tears at all times. If your eyes got dry, you'd go blind. Tears keep eyes moist and help keep out dust. Tears come from glands behind the upper eyelids. They bathe the eyes and flow out through ducts. The tear ducts are drains in the corners of the eyes nearest the nose. They are hidden inside the lower eyelid. When you cry, you let out too many tears for the ducts to handle, so they overflow.

3. Why do you need tears?

   A to drain water from your nose

   B to help you cry

   C to keep your eyes moist and dust-free

   D to make your feelings strong

4. Where do tears come from?

   F drains in your nose

   G drains in the corner of the eyes

   H inside the lower eyelid

   J glands behind the upper eyelids

Apply

Read the paragraphs. Then answer the questions.

Two great Americans died on one Fourth of July. It happened in 1826. People all over the United States were celebrating Independence Day. Then the news came. The country mourned the death of the two men. One was John Adams, the second president of the United States. The other was Thomas Jefferson, the third president. Both had worked hard to win freedom from British rule. Jefferson wrote the Declaration of Independence. Both Adams and Jefferson signed it. Both had been fine leaders in the new country. They had become close friends. And they died on the same day.

1. What happened on July 4, 1826?

   _____

2. How do you know that both Adams and Jefferson were important in the history of the United States?

   _____

3. Who wrote the Declaration of Independence?

   _____

People eat a lot of grass. But the grass they eat is not the same as lawn grass. Grains are type of grass. Oats, barley, corn, and wheat are all types of grass. Every bowl of cereal and loaf of bread is made from grasses. These grains have lots of vitamins and fiber. They are also big energy producers.

4. What kinds of grass do people eat?

   _____

5. Why are grains good to eat?

   _____

Check Up

Read the paragraph. Then circle the answer for each question.

Don't let the fragile look of a spiderweb fool you. The fiber that a spider uses in its web is the strongest for its size of any natural fiber. The Brazilian spider makes the strongest web of all. In Brazil, these webs can be found hanging between trees. They are often larger in diameter than the tire of a car. Four or five threads hold the webs to the trees. These are the strongest threads of all. People have sometimes walked into these webs without seeing them. They learned the hard way to avoid Brazilian spiderwebs. The threads cut into human skin like thin wires.

1. Which of the following is stated?

   A The Brazilian spider makes the strongest web of all.

   B Spiderwebs trap flies and insects.

   C A spiderweb is beautiful.

   D All spiderwebs are hard to see.

2. Which of the following is **not** stated?

   F Webs of the Brazilian spider can be found hanging between trees.

   G Webs of the Brazilian spider can be larger in diameter than the tire of a car.

   H People who walk into these webs by accident learn the hard way to avoid them.

   J Natural fibers are stronger than man-made fibers.

3. Listed below are important facts about spiderwebs. Which one is stated in this paragraph?

   A The fiber of a spiderweb is sticky.

   B A spider uses two kinds of thread for its web.

   C The fiber of a spiderweb is the strongest natural fiber there is.

   D Spiders themselves can get stuck on their webs, but they have a special way to free themselves.

4. Why should people avoid Brazilian spiderwebs, according to the statements in the paragraph?

   F The webs are huge.

   G The web fibers can cut skin.

   H They can't see the webs.

   J The webs hang between trees.

Read On Read "The Great Seal of the United States." Look for the stated concepts as you read. Then answer the questions.

Review

Details

Details support the **main idea** of a paragraph. The main idea of the paragraph below is the first sentence. The supporting details are underlined.

Charles Kettering made it easier for people to drive cars. When cars were first made, they were started with a hand crank The crank was on the front of the car. It took strength to start the crank. But in 1911 Kettering made starting cars easier. He invented the electric automobile self-starter.

Sequence

Sequence is the order in which events happen in a story. The underlined words in the paragraph below help to show sequence.

Our family grows tomatoes in our garden. First we plant tomatoes in the spring. All through the summer, we water and weed the tomatoes. Then we eat the first tomatoes in August. Finally, we can tomatoes in the fall.

Stated Concepts

One way to recall what you read is to note the facts and concepts that are stated. The **stated concepts** in the paragraph below are underlined.

The mayfly lives for more than three years but flies for only a day—its last. The mayfly spends most of its life burrowed in mud, as a larva. It spends its time eating and growing. When it matures, the larva sheds its skin. It has wings. Then it flies in the air and mates. After laying eggs, the mayfly dies. This often happens in one day, after three years of being a larva. The mayfly's adult stage is so short that it doesn't need to eat. Therefore, adult mayflies have no mouths.

Assessment

Read the paragraphs. Then circle the response that answers the question or completes the statement.

Blood donors are needed all the time. Over 12 million pints of blood are used each year in the United States. Blood donors save lives. But if you gave blood last year or even last month, it may not be of help to anyone today. Whole blood can be refrigerated and stored for 21 to 49 days. Plasma, red bloods cells, and other blood components can be frozen and stored for several years.

1. How many pints of blood are used each year in the United States?

   A over 12 million pints

   B over 21 million pints

   C over 49 million pints

   D not stated

2. Blood stays fresh

   F for 12 years

   G indefinitely

   H 21 to 49 days

   J for one year

Glass is one of the most useful materials in the world. It is made from silica sand, soda ash, and limestone. These materials are weighed and mixed in the right order. Then recycled or waste glass called *cullet* is added. Using cullet reduces the amount of heat needed to melt the new raw materials. Most glass is heated in large furnaces.

3. Which raw material is **not** used to make glass?

   A limestone

   B charcoal

   C silica sand

   D soda ash

4. Adding cullet to the new batch of glass

   F reduces the amount of heat needed to melt raw materials

   G makes the new glass stronger

   H adds color to the new batch

   J not stated

One of the chief sources of water pollution is industrial wastes. Some factories dump chemicals into the water. The burning of fossil fuels by power plants and cars releases oxides into the air. These oxides cause acid rain, which enters streams and lakes. Some industries pollute water another way. They use water to cool equipment. Heat from the equipment heats the water. The hot water is dumped into lakes and rivers. This heated water harms plants and animals. It is known as thermal pollution.

5. Acid rain is caused by

   A burning fossil fuels

   B heating water

   C dumping chemicals into lakes and rivers

   D combining chemicals in factories

6. Why is thermal pollution harmful?

   F It interferes with fish growth.

   G It harms water plants.

   H It wastes power.

   J not stated

   Arthur Ashe was a world-famous tennis player. He was the first African American to win the U.S. Men's National singles championship. He won that title in 1968. In 1975 Ashe became the first black man to win the Wimbledon singles match in England. Ashe was born in Richmond, Virginia, in 1943. As a college student, he won both the NCAA singles and doubles championships in 1966. He retired from tennis in 1980. Ashe died in 1993.

7. Which of these titles did Arthur Ashe win last?

   A Wimbledon singles

   B NCAA doubles

   C NCAA singles

   D U.S. men's singles

8. Ashe retired from tennis in

   F 1975

   G 1993

   H 1968

   J 1980

An almanac has many kinds of information. An almanac may have a calendar. It tells about important dates and events. It has facts about government and history. It also has facts about weather. Ben Franklin published *Poor Richard's Almanac* in 1722. It is well known for Franklin's many proverbs.

9. How often is an almanac published?

   A once a month

   B every ten years

   C once a year

   D not stated

10. *Poor Richard's Almanac* is well known for

    F Franklin's proverbs

    G accurate weather predictions

    H geographical facts

    J news about annual events

Elephants have tender skin. Most people think that an elephant's skin is tough as leather. It may look tough, but it isn't. Elephants hate the insects that nibble on their hides. Their skin is so tender that they feel every bite. The sun also bothers them. But elephants have several ways of staying comfortable. Lying in the mud helps soothe their itchy skin. Hay tossed over their shoulders makes a great back scratcher. They also like to take showers. Elephants cool off their backs with a stream of water that they shoot from their trunks.

11. An elephant tosses hay over its shoulder

    A to play with its food

    B to scare off its enemies

    C to scratch its back

    D to make a bed

12. When cooling itself off, an elephant uses its trunk as

    F a fan

    G a hose

    H a spoon

    J hook

Diagrams

Many articles have diagrams that show how things are made or how they work. Diagrams may use arrows to show direction, and they may have captions.

Study the following diagram. This diagram shows how a broadcast signal gets from a far-away station to your home.

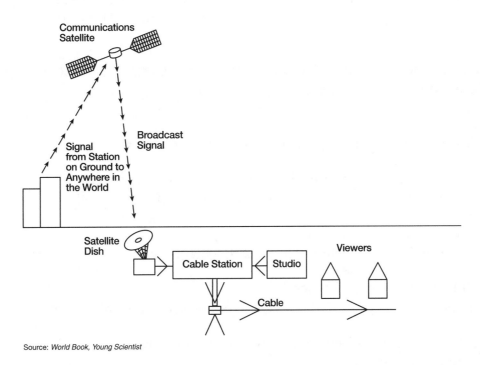

Source: *World Book, Young Scientist*

1. Where does the broadcast signal first come from?

   _____

2. What object sends the signal to the satellite dish?

   _____

3. Where does the satellite dish send the signal?

   _____

4. How does the cable station send the signal to viewers?

   _____

Identifying Goals

Sometimes in our busy lives it is necessary to identify and set goals. Goals should be stated exactly. Tell what you plan to do and how you plan to do it. You should also decide when you will meet the goal.

Goal: Pay off a $1,000 loan in 24 months so that I owe no one money.

Exact goal: pay off $1,000 loan
Measure of goal: owing no more money
Length of time: 24 months

In each pair of sentences, underline the sentence that states a goal that is specific and identifies when and how the goal will be reached.

1. Take a trip to Mexico someday.
   Fly to Mexico with my family in January to visit relatives.

2. Save $1,300 this year by putting $25 a week into a savings account.
   Save some extra money from my paycheck if I can after I pay bills.

3. Learn how to use my new computer.
   Take computer lessons one night a week to learn how to use my computer.

4. Spend time with my grandfather.
   Have lunch with my grandfather every Wednesday at a local restaurant.

5. Paint the living room before the family reunion in July.
   Fix up the house, which is a mess.

6. Join the Running Club and exercise on machines twice a week.
   Get in shape.

7. Write a goal you have. It should tell exactly what you will do, when you will do it, and how you will do it.

   _____

   _____

   _____

   _____

   _____

Reading Graphs

Graphs are an easy way to give information. You will find graphs in newspapers and magazines.

Bar graphs are used to make comparisons. First, read the title of the graph. Then look at its labels.

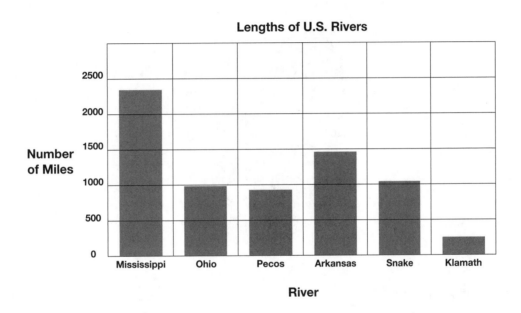

1. What is the title of the graph? _____

2. What does each bar tell you? _____

3. What counting pattern do you see in this graph? _____

4. Which river listed is the longest? _____

5. Which river listed is the shortest? _____

6. Which would go farther, a boat going down the Ohio River from beginning to end

   or one going down the Snake River? _____

Practice

A **circle graph** shows what part of a whole thing each part makes up. The whole circle represents 100 percent, and the sections show the percentage of each part.

Look at the circle graph and answer the questions.

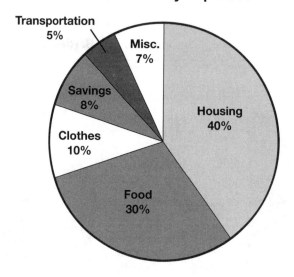

Jackson Family Expenses

1. What is the graph about? _____

2. What does each section show? _____

3. In which category does the family spend the most money?

   _____

4. In which category does the family spend the least amount of money?

   _____

5. In which category does the family spend 7% of their expenses?

   _____

6. In which category does the family spend twice as much as they do on

   transportation? _____

7. What percentage of the family's expenses is spent on both food and housing

   together? _____

Apply

A **line graph** is often used to show changes over time.

Look at the line graph below and answer the questions that follow.

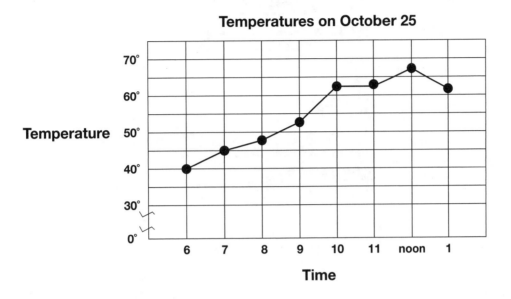

Temperatures on October 25

1. What is shown from left to right on the graph? _____

2. What is shown from top to bottom on the graph? _____

3. What does the graph compare? _____

4. About what temperature was it at 9 A.M.? _____

5. At what time of day was the highest temperature reached? _____

6. Between which two times did the temperatures increase the most? _____

Check Up

Read the graph. Then circle the answer for each question.

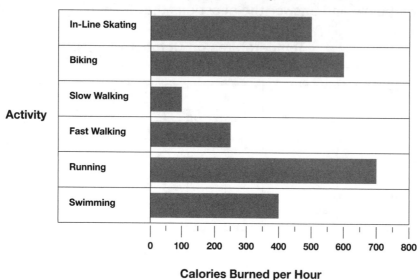

Calories Used in Sports Activities

1. What kind of graph is this?

   A line graph

   B circle graph

   C bar graph

   D pie chart

2. Which activity burns the most calories?

   F biking

   G swimming

   H fast walking

   J running

3. How many calories are burned in one hour of fast walking?

   A 600

   B 300

   C 250

   D 200

4. How many calories could you burn by in-line skating for two hours?

   F 250

   G 500

   H 750

   J 1000

5. Which activity burns four times the number of calories per hour as slow walking?

   A swimming

   B fast walking

   C running

   D biking

Reading Maps

A **map** is a drawing that shows places. Different maps show different types of information. A **political map** shows boundaries, countries, and cities. A **road map** shows highways and other roads. A **weather map** shows temperatures and other weather information. A **contour map** can show elevation, or distance above sea level.

Look at the map. Then answer the questions.

1. Is this a road map or a political map?

   _____

2. What area does the map show?

   _____

3. What direction does State Highway 255 run?

   _____

4. What points of interest are shown?

   _____

5. What is another name for State Highway 255?

   _____

6. Do Neal Road and Martin Road cross one another?

   _____

7. What river does Martin Road cross?

   _____

8. About how far is it from Westlawn to the U.S. Army Missile Command?

   _____

Huntsville, Alabama

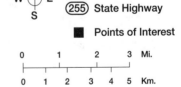

Practice

Maps are used to show a variety of information. In order to read and understand a map, you need to look at its **legend**. A legend is a chart that explains the symbols used on a map.

Look at the map and legend below and answer the questions.

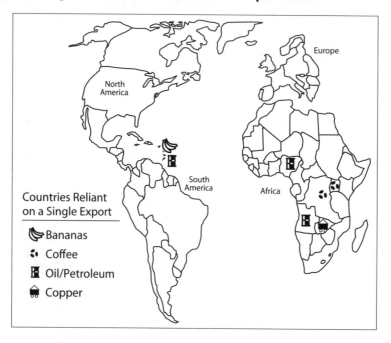

1. What does the legend show? _____

   _____

2. Which four continents are shown on the map? _____

   _____

3. On which continent does a country rely on copper as its single export?

   _____

4. Which product do most countries rely on as a single export?

   _____

5. How many countries rely on coffee as a single export?

   _____

6. Which product(s) do countries in North America rely on as a single export?

   _____

Apply

A **mileage map** can show distances between cities. People who travel might use a mileage map to plan their trips.

Use the mileage map below to answer the questions.

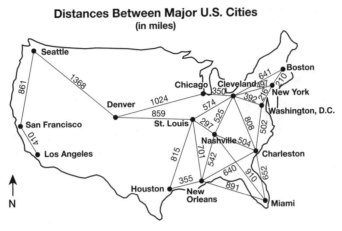

Distances Between Major U.S. Cities
(in miles)

1. About how far is it between Seattle and Denver?

   _____

2. Which city named on the map is closest to Cleveland?

   _____

3. About how far is it from Los Angeles to Seattle?

   _____

4. Which route is shorter between Cleveland and Miami—the one through Nashville

   or the one through Charleston? _____

5. Through which cities would you travel to make the shortest trip possible from New

   Orleans to Boston? _____

6. If you travel 400 miles a day, about how long will it take to go from Houston to

   St. Louis? _____

7. If you drive from New Orleans to Miami, would you drive more or less than 891

   miles? Why? _____

Check Up

Look at the map. Then circle the answer for each question.

Olympia, Washington

⑤ Interstate Highway

⑩⑪ U.S. Highway

■ Points of Interest

N
W ⊕ E
S

0   1 Mi.
0   1   Km.

1. What city is the focus of this map?

   A Lacey

   B Olympia

   C Tumwater

   D Chambers Lake

2. What direction is Olympia from Lacey?

   F north

   G south

   H east

   J west

3. What river does Interstate Highway 5 cross?

   A Percival River

   B Woodard River

   C Indian River

   D The highway doesn't cross a river.

4. About how many miles is it from Martin Way to Log Cabin Road?

   F 1 mile

   G 2 miles

   H 3 miles

   J 6 miles

5. What direction is Little League Baseball Park from Chambers Lake?

   A west

   B south

   C northwest

   D southwest

Read On   Read "The Channel Under the Sea." Then answer the questions about graphic information.

Using Forms

You fill out a **form** to provide information about yourself. You may fill out a form for many reasons. For example, when you apply for a job, you may have to fill out a form.

Forms often use short phrases or abbreviations when asking for information. It is important to understand these phrases or abbreviations. Then you can complete the form correctly.

The form below is part of an application for a credit card. Do not fill out the form. Instead, answer the questions that follow.

(Please Print)			
Name		SS#	
Street Address			
City	State	Zip Code	
Years There	Own/Rent		
Annual Income $_____			

1. What does the abbreviation SS# stand for?

   _____

2. Why does the form request that you print the information?

   _____

3. If you make about $2,000 a month, what amount should you write for your annual

   income? _____

Practice

Here is part of a job application form. Look at the form. Answer the questions about it.

(1)_____		
Name		
(2)_____		
Street Address		
(3)_____		
City	State	Zip Code
(4)_____		
Position Applying For	Desired Salary	When Available?
(5)_____		
High School	Year of Graduation	
(6)_____		
College	Degree	Year
(7)_____		
Other Education		
(8)_____		
Computer Skills and Experience		
(9)_____		
Computer Programs		

1. What information should you put in the Desired Salary section?

   _____

2. What is the question *When Available?* asking?

   _____

3. What year is being asked for in item 6?

   _____

4. Agnes is applying for a job as a cook in a restaurant. She recently went to a workshop called Cooking for Large Groups. Where on the form should she put this information?

   _____

Apply

This is part of an application for health insurance. Study the form. Answer the questions about it.

22.	Ht. _____ Wt. _____ Ht. _____ Wt. _____ Proposed Insured Spouse
23.	Has Weight Changed More Than 10 Pounds in Last Year? Proposed Insured Yes No Spouse Yes No
24.	Ever Smoked? Proposed Insured Yes No Spouse Yes No
25.	Last Doctor Consultation: Proposed Insured _____ Spouse _____ Reason: Proposed Insured _____ Spouse _____

1. Who is *proposed insured?* _____

2. Who is *spouse?* _____

3. What should the applicant do if he or she is not sure of weight?

_____

4. What should the applicant do with the words *Yes* and *No* on the form?

_____

Check Up

Look at the form. Do not fill it out. Answer the questions that follow.

```
BILL TO:                                    SHIP TO: (Only if different from "Bill to.")
Name _____             First Name _____
Address _____            Last Name _____
_____            Address _____
City _____                                  _____
State _____ Zip _____ Country _____       City _____
Phone Number _____             State _____ Zip _____ Country _____

Item Number   Page   Description            Size    Color    Qty.    Price
_____  _____  _____        _____  _____  _____  _____
_____  _____  _____        _____  _____  _____  _____

                                                   Total prices        _____

                                                   Sales tax           _____
Method of Payment
Check or money order enclosed _____            TOTAL               _____
Charge to my (check one):
Visa _____   MasterCard _____   American Express _____
Credit Card Number _____      Expiration Date: Month _____ Year _____

Signature (as shown on credit card)
```

1. When might you need to fill out a
    form like this?

    A if you are placing a catalog order
    by phone

    B if you are placing a catalog order
    by mail

    C if you are sending a package out
    of town

    D if you want something charged to
    a credit card

2. What should you put under *Qty*?

    F the number of quarts of
    something you are ordering

    G the number of items that you
    want to buy described in the row

    H a ✔ to indicate that you want the
    best quality available

    J an asterisk if you are going to
    write a special note below

3. When would you need to fill out the
    "Ship To" section?

    A if you want the company to send
    your order instead of you picking
    it up

    B if you want the order shipped to
    another country

    C if your shipping address is the
    same as your billing address

    D if your shipping address is
    different from your billing address

Using Schedules

A **schedule** is a chart or table that lists when events take place. A bus schedule, for example, gives the times when the bus will be at each stop along its route. A television schedule tells when certain programs will be broadcast on each channel.

Look at this train schedule. Use it to answer the questions that follow.

Station	Madison	Dearborn	Franklin	Pierce
6:30 A.M.	6:37	6:42	6:50	7:02
6:45 A.M.	. . . .	. . . .	7:05	7:17
7:00 A.M.	7:07	7:12	7:20	7:32

1. Is this a schedule for the morning trains or the evening trains?

   _____

2. How often do the trains leave the station?

   _____

3. How long does it take the 6:45 train to get from the station to the Franklin stop?

   _____

4. If you needed to be at Franklin by 7:00 A.M., which train would you have to catch

   from the station? _____

5. If you miss the 6:30 A.M. train from the station, what is the earliest you could get to

   Dearborn? _____

6. If you took the 7:00 A.M. train from the station, what time would you get to Pierce?

   _____

7. What does the line of dots under the Madison and Dearborn stops mean?

   _____

8. If you wanted to be at Madison by 7:00 A.M., which train would you have to take

   from the station? _____

Practice

Check the television schedule below. Answer the questions that follow.

	2 CBS	4 NBC	6 ABC	8 PBS	9 WGN	CNN	ESPN
7:30	Can't Stop Laughin'	24 Hours	News Special	Patty's Pet Parade	Baseball's Game of the Week	Early News	Prairie Golf Tournament
8:00	The Trauma Team	Top Favorite Movies	//////// ////////	Astronomers' Circle	//////// ////////	This Year in Politics	//////// ////////
8:30	Ned's Neighbors	//////// ////////	The Multi-Millionaire Quiz	//////// ////////	//////// ////////	//////// ////////	Soccer Highlights
9:00	Kay Winters, Private Eye	//////// ////////	//////// ////////	A Tour of China	//////// ////////	World Economy	Meet the Players
9:30	//////// ////////	//////// ////////	Spin a Word	//////// ////////	News	//////// ////////	//////// ////////
10:00	News	News	News	Civil War Chronicles (R)	Amazing Animals (R)	News	Pro Sports Wrap-Up

1. How many TV stations are listed on this schedule? _____

2. In this schedule, what does / / / / / / / / / mean?

   _____

3. If you wanted to watch sports at 7:30, what would be your choices?

   _____

4. According to this schedule, which station has game shows on tonight?

   _____

5. If you enjoy politics, which program could you watch tonight?

   _____

6. Suppose your young children want to watch TV at 7:30. Which program or programs might they enjoy? _____

7. Which stations do not have news on at 10?

   _____

8. If you start to watch TV at 9 and don't like to start in the middle of a program, what would be your choices?

   _____

Apply

Here is part of an airline departure schedule. Answer the following questions about it.

Flight	Destination	Departures Scheduled	Will Depart	Gate
117	Chicago	2:30 P.M.	On Time	15A
243	Chicago	3:05 P.M.	On Time	15B
302	Kansas City	2:45 P.M.	Delayed	16
123	Phoenix	2:51 P.M.	On Time	18
209	Los Angeles	2:55 P.M.	On Time	22
447	San Diego	3:02 P.M.	3:15 P.M.	24
322	Denver	3:17 P.M.	On Time	15A

1. When does Flight 117 leave? _____

2. At what time was the flight to Kansas City scheduled to

   leave? _____

3. From what gate does Flight 209 depart? _____

4. For what flight are the people at Gate 18 waiting?

   _____

5. At what time will the flight to San Diego leave?

   _____

6. Which flights will not depart on time?

   _____

7. Suppose you are taking the last flight to Chicago. What is your flight number?

   _____

8. If you get on a flight from Gate 15A at 2:30, where are you going?

   _____

Check Up

Look at the baseball schedule. Circle the response that answers each question or completes each sentence.

**Badgers Little League
June Game Schedule**

Fri	Sat	Sun
2 Cubbies 7 P.M.	3 H Pirates 4 P.M.	4 H Reds 3:30 P.M.
9 H Sox 7 P.M.	10 H Cougars 4 P.M.	11 Pirates 3:30 P.M.
16 H Cubbies 7 P.M.	17 H Cubbies 4 P.M.	18
23 Sox 7 P.M.	24 Sox 7 P.M.	25 Cougars 3:30 P.M.
30 H Cubbies 7 P.M.		

H—Home game; all others are away

1. This is the schedule for which team?

   A Badgers

   B Cubbies

   C Cougars

   D Sox

2. What does the number in the upper left corner of each square represent?

   F the games played

   G number of runs

   H the date in June

   J the date in July

3. On June 16 the Badgers play the

   A Cougars

   B Sox

   C Reds

   D Cubbies

4. The Badgers play the

   F Cubbies at 6 P.M. on June 16

   G Reds at 7 P.M. on June 21

   H Cougars at home at 3:30 P.M. on June 26

   J Sox at home at 7 P.M. on June 9

5. At 7 P.M. on June 23,

   A the Badgers will play the Sox away

   B the Badgers will play the Sox at home

   C the Sox will play the Cougars at home

   D there will be no game

Read On   Read "Do You Have the Time?" Then answer the questions about forms and schedules.

Using Indexes

A book's **index** is at the back of the book. It lists names, topics, and important terms that are mentioned in the book. **Entries** are listed alphabetically. Each page in the book where the subject is discussed is listed.

Sometimes a book has a lot of information about a topic. In that case, the index also lists **subentries**.

Below is the beginning of the index for a book called *World Mythology*.

African myths
    of creation, 425–431
    of the epic hero, 444–452
    of fertility, 431–434
American myths
    of creation, 456–463, 488–494
    of divine heroes, 457, 499–502
Aphrodite. *See* Venus

Babylonian myths, 156
Badger, as mythical character, 493
Beowulf, 289–310
Bifrost Bridge, 224

Boreas, the North Wind, 25
Brutus, in *King Arthur*, 313
Bull of Heaven, in *Gilgamesh*, 199–204, 213

Caesar, Augustus, 133, 125
Caesar, Julius, 118–119, 146
Carthage, 117
Celts, 274
Centaurs, 144
Ceres. *See* Demeter
Chanson de Roland, 311
Charybdis, 97–100, 136

Use the index from this book about mythology to answer each question.

1. On what pages would you find information about African myths?

   _____

2. Which two entries give information about creation myths?

   _____

3. What topic is discussed on page 144?

   _____

4. If you are interested in the goddess Aphrodite, under what entry would you look?

   _____

5. On what page would you find information about Brutus in the King Arthur legend?

   _____

Practice

Some indexes give additional information. In the index below, titles of paintings, drawings, and other artwork are in italic type. This is a brief section of an index for a book called *Art History*.

Cassatt, Mary, 1005, 1013–1014; *pictures*, 1013, 1017
castles, Gothic, 561–565, 578-79; *picture*, 579
catacombs, 291–292, 294; See also *glossary*
Catharina Hooft and Her Nurse, by Frans Hals, 787
cave art, 41–46, 135
    dating of, 46, 49
Cellini, Benvenuto, 722–723; *Saltcellar of Francis I*, 723
ceramics
    African, 925
    Chinese, 363; *pictures*, 57
    contemporary, 1163–1164
    Greek, 162
    Islamic, 348, 353, 357

Use the index above to decide if each statement is *true* or *false*. If it is false, explain why.

1. Mary Cassatt was an artist.

    true   false

_____

2. There is a picture of a Gothic castle on page 579.

    true   false

_____

3. Catacombs are defined in the glossary.

    true   false

_____

4. The painting called *Catharina Hooft and Her Nurse* is by Benvenuto Cellini.

    true   false

_____

5. You can find pictures of African ceramics on page 57.

    true   false

_____

Apply

Some magazines have an index at the back that tells you what subjects that issue covers. Magazines sometimes include an index in their December issue of all the articles they have published all year, showing their titles and authors and where they were published (month and page number). These indexes are alphabetized by the first important word in the title. For example, "The Information Economy" is alphabetized under "I" for *Information*.

Look at the *Scientific American* index. Answer the questions that follow.

"Industrial Ecology of the 21st Century, The." Robert A. Frosch; Sept., p. 178

"Infinity, A Brief History of." A. W. Moore; April, p. 112

"Information Economy, The." Hal R. Varian; Sept., p. 200

"Intelligent Software," Pattie Maes; Sept., p. 84

"Juggling: It's a Science," Peter J. Beek and Arthur Lewbel; Nov., p. 92

"Laser Control of Chemical Reactions." Paul Bremer and Moshe Shapiro; March, p. 56

"Machines That Learn from Hints." Yaser S. Abu-Mostafa; April, p. 64

"Magnets, Building World-Record." Greg Boebinger, Al Passner, and Joze Bevk; June, p. 58

"Manic-Depressive Illness and Creativity." Kay Redfield Jamison; Feb., p. 62

"Mesopotamian City: A Tapestry of Power." Elizabeth C. Stone and Paul Zimansky; April, p. 118

"Microprocessors in 2020." David A. Patterson; Sept., p. 62

"Microscopic Machines." Kaigham J. Gabriel; Sept., p. 150

"Nuclear War." Philip Morrison; Aug, p. 42

"Ocean's Midwaters." Bruce H. Robison; July, p. 60

"Population, Poverty, and the Local Environment." Partha S. Dasgupta; Feb., p. 40

1. In what issue would you find an article about intelligent software?

_____

2. How many authors cowrote the article about magnets? _____

3. On what page of the March issue does the laser article start? _____

4. Which article involves a prediction about microprocessors?_____

5. In what issue does the article "Nuclear War" appear? _____

6. Who wrote the article about manic depression? _____

Check Up

Read the index to *The Human Body*. Circle the answer to each question.

Ears
    auditory canals, 276-289; *picture*, 289
    auditory nerves, 276
    bones. *See* Ossicles
    eardrum, 287, 290; *picture*, 280
    See also inner ear; middle ear
Eggs, human. *See* Ova
Elderly, 245-259

Electroencephalograms (EEGs), 36, 85-90;
    picture, 88
Endocrine glands, 235, 239; *picture*, 238
    See also Adrenal glands; Hormones;
    Pancreas; Pituitary gland; Thymus;
    Thyroid gland

1. On what page would you find a picture of an eardrum?

   A 289

   B 287

   C 280

   D 276

2. What are ova?

   F ossicles

   G bones

   H humans

   J eggs

3. What would you find on page 85?

   A information about EEGs

   B information about endocrine glands

   C a picture of an EEG

   D a picture of an endocrine gland

4. On what pages would you find information about elderly people?

   F 245

   G 259

   H 245 and 259

   J 245 through 259

5. Under what entry should you look for more information about endocrine glands?

   A EEGs

   B auditory canals

   C pancreas

   D ossicles

6. Which entry does **not** have a picture?

   F ears

   G elderly

   H EEGs

   J endocrine glands

7. The word *auditory* is about

   A nerves

   B bones

   C hearing

   D seeing

8. Where could you look for information about the bones in your foot?

   F under "ossicles"

   G under the subentry "inner ear"

   H under the main entry "bones"

   J under "EEGs"

Understanding Consumer Materials

We are all consumers. We buy things that we need or want. To make good buying decisions, consumers should understand **consumer materials,** such as advertisements.

Look at the advertisement. Answer the questions that follow.

1,200 wireless phone service minutes for only $29.99*

(200 weekday and 1,000 weekend minutes)

Go Ahead! Burn Up Your Minutes!
The NEW QXR-307 by Magnulux

$49.99

-$50.00 with instant rebate

FREE!

Hurry! Offer ends October 31, 2002!

*Requires a one-year service agreement

---

1. What is this ad trying to sell?

   _____

2. Why does the ad say you can "Burn up your minutes"?

   _____

3. What does the asterisk (*) after $29.99 mean? _____

   _____

4. Why are the words "1,200 wireless phone service minutes for only $29.99" and "FREE" the largest words in the ad?

   _____

5. Why is the sentence "Requires a one-year service agreement" written in small letters and placed at the bottom of the ad?

   _____

Practice

Following is information you might see in an ad for an expensive item. Read the information carefully. Answer the questions that follow.

NO monthly payments!
NO finance charges
for one full year!*
If paid in full per terms below.

*Subject to credit approval. Applies to purchases of $1000 or more with minimum 25% down payment on dealer credit card plan. Finance charges will accrue but will not be imposed if balance is paid in full prior to one year from date of purchase. If not, finance charges will be assessed from date of purchase. Variable APR (annual percentage rate) is prime rate + 9.9%. (Minimum APR 13.8%.)

---

1. What do you have to do to avoid paying finance charges?

   _____

2. Why does a company advertise "No finance charges for one full year" if that is only true under certain conditions?

   _____

3. What does "subject to credit approval" mean?

   _____

4. Why do you think the store insists you use the "dealer credit card plan" instead of your own credit card?

   _____

5. Suppose you made a purchase under this agreement on March 13, 2002. If you pay the balance in full on April 1, 2003, will you have to pay interest? Why or why not?

   _____

   _____

Apply

Advertisers are trying to sell you products or services. Before you buy, you want to ask yourself questions such as What is being sold? What does the ad promise? Can the promises be met? Is the cost fair? Can I return the product and get my money back?

Read the following ad. Then answer the questions.

> "*Seven Steps to Seven Million* has changed my life!" Tony Johnson says, "This book has made me a wealthy man, and it can do the same for you."
>
> Change your life as Tony has changed his! Join the thousands who have turned themselves from losers into winners!
>
> Just $29.95! A surprise bonus for everyone who orders before October 30!
>
> Fill out the order form below NOW and send just $29.95 plus shipping and handling.

1. What does this ad seem to be promising in the first paragraph?

   _____

2. What is the second paragraph trying to make readers think will happen if they buy

   this book? _____

3. What type of person do you think this ad is designed to appeal to?

   _____

4. Why do you think the company promises a surprise bonus with orders received

   before October 30? _____

5. Do you know for sure, after reading the ad, that Tony Johnson made $7 million as a

   result of reading the book?_____

6. If this ad interests you, what could you do to find out more about the book before

   buying it? _____

Check Up

Read the advertisement below. Circle the response that answers each question or completes each sentence.

Summer Food Celebration!

Come to the Marvelous Market NOW for the best prices on the freshest foods!

Take advantage of our specials!
Eggs 50¢ a dozen!
Marvelous Brand bread just 49¢!

Guaranteed lowest prices!

We're so sure that our prices are the lowest that we offer this incredible guarantee: Marvelous Market will refund DOUBLE THE DIFFERENCE between our price and any local store's advertised price for the identical item.

---

1. The main point of the ad is that you should shop at Marvelous Market because it has

   A the best selection

   B the lowest prices

   C fresh food

   D a convenient location

2. What reason does the ad give for why you should go to the store NOW?

   F to take advantage of the specials

   G to get eggs before they sell out

   H to take advantage of the limited guarantee

   J to take part in the celebration

3. Suppose you bought the Marvelous Market eggs for 50¢ a dozen and found an ad for a dozen eggs at a competing store for 45¢. How much of a refund would you get?

   A 5¢

   B 10¢

   C 90¢

   D $1.00

4. The bread is advertised for 49¢. What is the most likely reason for selling it at that price?

   F The bread is stale.

   G The loaves are smaller than usual.

   H The store hopes that people will come in to buy bread and end up buying lots of other things.

   J Customers don't like the bread.

Using Consumer Materials

Consumers enter into **contracts** all the time. Sometimes they do not realize they have made a contract. For example, if you have a credit card or a bank account, you have entered into a contract. Following is part of a **lease** for an apartment. A lease is a contract that describes in detail the responsibilities of both the renter and the landlord. Study the lease. Answer the questions.

> This lease covers the property at 1417 Lee Street, Apartment 10C, in Lake Forest, Indiana. The property is to be used and occupied by Lessee as a residence and for no other purpose from September 1, 2003 to August 31, 2004.
>
> RENT. Monthly rent of $950.00 shall be paid by Lessee to Lessor. It is due on or before the first day of every month. A penalty of $100 shall be fined by Lessor against Lessee for each and every rent payment more than five (5) business days late.
>
> SECURITY DEPOSIT. On signing the lease, Lessee makes a security deposit of $1500. The deposit will be returned with four percent (4%) interest if the apartment is in good condition when the lease ends and is not renewed.

1. Who is the Lessee? _____

2. Could the person who signs this lease run a sewing business out of the apartment? Why or why not? _____

3. What is the minimum amount the renter will have to pay on the day the lease is signed? _____

4. What happens if the rent is paid more than 5 business days late?

   _____

5. If rent is due on Wednesday, March 1, and it is not paid until Tuesday, March 7, does the penalty have to be paid? Why or why not?

   _____

6. When does the Lessee get his or her security deposit back?

   _____

Practice

Credit card companies sometimes send letters to people. The companies want people to sign up for their credit cards. The chart shown is printed in small type on the back of one such letter. Read the parts of the letter shown. Then answer the questions.

Take advantage of our credit card!

Put all your credit charges on one card. You will enjoy an APR (annual percentage rate) as low as 2.9%* on transferred balances for six months. Monthly payments must be made to keep this low rate. Transfer your balances from other credit cards to ours! See how much you save!

*Annual Percentage Rate	Promotional rate of 2.9% for 6 months if you transfer balances of $4,000 or more; 3.9% if you transfer balances of less than $3,500. Rate for new purchases: 13.9% Rate for cash advances: 19.99% If you default, rate increases to 23.99%
Variable Rate Information	The annual percentage rate for purchases may vary monthly. We calculate the rate by adding 4.4% to the U.S. Prime Rate published by the *Wall Street Journal* on the last business day of each month. That rate currently is 9.5%.

1. What are "transferred balances"?

   _____

2. If you transferred a balance of $2,000 from another credit card, what rate of interest would you pay on this balance?

   _____

3. Why is this chart printed in small type on the back of the letter?

   _____

   _____

4. What symbol found in the claim about the APR means that details about the claim are somewhere else in the letter?

   _____

5. What interest rate do you pay on new purchases made with this card?

   _____

Apply

Almost any appliance you buy comes with an **owner's manual**. The manual explains how to use and take care of the appliance.

Read the following portion of an owner's manual for a cordless telephone. Then answer the questions.

The Battery Pack

If the light does not go on when you put the handset on the base, the battery pack and the AC adapter may not be connected properly. It is also possible that the charging contacts on the base and on the handset need to be cleaned. Do this with an ordinary pencil eraser.

About once a month, discharge the battery fully to maintain its ability to fully recharge. Leaving the handset off the base until the LOW indicator flashes will discharge the battery.

Recharge the battery whenever the LOW indicator flashes. Place the handset on the base for several hours or overnight.

1. How can you tell when it is time to recharge the battery?

   _____

2. Why should you discharge the battery?

   _____

3. How do you discharge the battery completely?

   _____

4. If you put the handset on the base to recharge the battery and the light does not go on, what could be wrong?

   _____

5. If you put the handset on the base to recharge the battery and the light does not go on, what should you do?

   _____

   _____

Check Up

Study this nutrition table from a box of cereal. Refer to it to answer the questions.

Nutrition Facts	
Serving Size 1 Cup (54 g/1.9 oz.)	
Servings Per Container About 9	
Amount Per Serving	**Cereal**
Calories	190
Calories from fat	10
Total Fat 1g	2%
Saturated Fat 0 g	0%
Cholesterol 0 mg	0%
Sodium 5 mg	0%
Potassium 210 mg	6%
Total	
Carbohydrate 44 g	15%
Dietary Fiber 5 g	24%
Sugars 9 g	
Other Carbohydrate 30 g	
Protein 5 g	
Vitamin A	10%
(100% as Beta-carotene)	
Vitamin C	0%
Ingredients: Whole grain wheat, brown sugar, whole oats, sugar, honey	

1. One serving of cereal is

   A 54 g + 1.9 oz.

   B 1 cup + 54 g + 1.9 oz.

   C 1 cup

   D 1 cup + 1.9 oz.

2. What does the letter *g* stand for?

   F grams

   G kilograms

   H gigabytes

   J milligrams

3. One serving of this cereal gives you about ¼ of your daily value of

   A potassium

   B dietary fiber

   C calories

   D beta-carotene

4. Of all the ingredients in this cereal, the one found in the highest percentage is

   F brown sugar

   G honey

   H whole grain wheat

   J brown rice

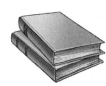

Read On   Read about contracts and other consumer materials in "The History of Money." Then answer the questions.

Review

Graphs

Using **graphs** is a way to give information quickly and easily. Graphs are often used to show comparisions. These comparisons can be shown on **bar graphs**, **circle graphs**, and **line graphs**.

Maps

Maps are drawings that show places. For example, a **political map** may show boundaries, countries, and cities. A **road map** shows highways and other roads. A **weather map** shows temperatures and other weather information. A **contour map** can show elevation, or distance above sea level.

Forms

Forms ask for information. You complete forms for many different reasons, such as obtaining a credit card, applying for a job, or paying taxes.

Schedules

Schedules show the times and places that events take place. You may need to read a train schedule, a bus schedule, or an airline schedule the next time you travel.

Indexes

A book's **index**, at the back of the book, lists alphabetically names, topics, and important terms that are mentioned in the book and gives their page numbers. If a book has a lot of information about a topic, the index also lists subentries.

Consumer Materials

Advertisements are the communications a company uses to provide information and to persuade **consumers** to buy products or services. To protect themselves, consumers must read and understand all information that companies give them.

Assessment

Look at the graphs and answer the questions.

Types of Recycled Materials

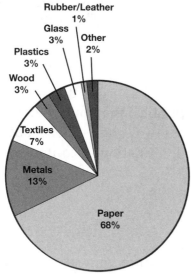

Source: U.S. Environmental Protection Agency

Percentage of Some Common Items Recycled

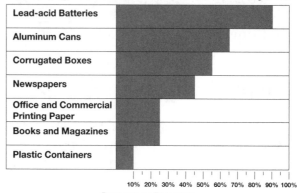

Source: U.S. Environmental Protection Agency

1. What is the graph about?

   A amounts of garbage produced by Americans

   B types of recycled materials

   C contents of landfills

   D cost of recycling

2. Which item makes up the largest percentage of recycled material?

   F metals

   G paper

   H wood

   J other

3. Which item makes up the smallest percentage of recycled material?

   A wood

   B plastics

   C rubber and leather

   D textiles

4. What percentage of newspapers is recycled?

   F 25%

   G 40%

   H 45%

   J 65%

5. Of which item is only 10% recycled?

   A aluminum cans

   B plastic containers

   C lead-acid batteries

   D glass containers

6. The percentage of books and magazines that is recycled is equal to the percentage of recycled

   _____.

   F office and commercial printing paper

   G glass containers

   H newspapers

   J corrugated boxes

Assessment continued

Look at the map and answer the questions.

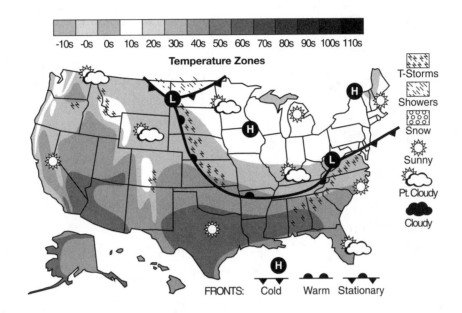

7. According to the map, what is the weather in Texas today?

   A sunny

   B thunderstorms

   C partly cloudy

   D cloudy

8. In what part of the country is the cold front?

   F northeast

   G north central

   H southwest

   J south central

9. What information is not given on the weather map?

   A temperature zones

   B fronts

   C locations of rainfall

   D wind speed

10. When applying for a credit card, what information probably would **not** be necessary?

    F bank name

    G address

    H children's names

    J saving account number

11. What information is included on a job application form?

    A spouse's job title

    B car registration number

    C work experience

    D shipping and handling charges

12. What information would **not** be needed on a mail-order form?

    F item number

    G sales tax

    H quantity

    J date of birth

Look at the consumer materials and answer the questions.

	Monday
Drafting	8:00-9:00
Algebra	11:00-12:00
U.S. History	2:00-3:30
English	5:00-6:00

Dial Anywhere Calling Plan	
Calling Plan	Anywhere Minutes (per month)
$17.99 per month	100
$31.99 per month	350
$42.99 per month	700

13. What class is held from 11:00 to 12:00 on Monday?

    A drafting

    B algebra

    C English

    D biology

14. How many classes are held on Monday?

    F 2

    G 3

    H 4

    J 6

15. Which class meets for more than one hour?

    A drafting

    B algebra

    C U.S. history

    D biology

16. How many anywhere minutes do you get with the $42.99 calling plan?

    F 100

    G 350

    H 500

    J 700

17. How many fewer anywhere minutes do you get with the $17.99 calling plan than with the $42.99 calling plan?

    A 600

    B 350

    C 800

    D 375

18. The words in an index are usually organized

    F in page number order

    G in alphabetical order

    H by date

    J by chapter

One-Word Descriptions

What is a character like? What word or words can you use to tell about a character? The words that describe a character are called **character traits**. Read each of the following words. Think of a character the word might describe. The character may be from a book you have read. Maybe it is someone you have seen on television or in the movies. Write the person's name. Share your answers with others.

proud _____	generous _____	dishonest _____
brave _____	friendly _____	smart _____
selfish _____	successful _____	stubborn _____

Choose one of the people you named. Write a paragraph that shows why you think he or she has that character trait.

_____

_____

_____

_____

_____

_____

_____

Seeing Both Sides

It is possible to look at every situation in different ways. Some people see the good side of a situation. Some people see the bad side of a situation. Read each statement in the chart. Write two sentences for each one. In one sentence, tell something positive, or good. In the other sentence, tell something negative, or bad. Sentences have been written for the first statement in the chart. Use these as examples.

Positive Side		Negative Side
Dolores likes to help other readers choose books.	Dolores works at the library.	Dolores has to work on weekends and until 9 o'clock at night.
	We ride the bus to school.	
	Last night it snowed.	
	I live in an apartment.	
	I am learning to play the piano.	

Recognizing Character Traits

Authors can make **characters** seem real to readers. They let the readers know what the character is like through the character's **words, thoughts, and actions**. Authors also show why characters act as they do and what they believe in by describing their actions, words, and thoughts. Sometimes authors show what characters are like in another way. They reveal a character through what others think and say about him or her.

Read each character's statement. Then circle the word that best describes the character.

1. "That's right! I won the raffle. It's my $100.00. I am not sharing it with you or anyone else. I'm using it to buy myself something. Don't even think about asking me for some of the money."

    A generous

    B angry

    C happy

    D selfish

2. "I had chores to do. Mom said to do them the first thing in the morning. These were my jobs. They helped the family. However, the day was beautiful. The sun was shining. My friends were going to the park. I wanted to go, too. The chores could wait, so I went to the park."

    F lazy

    G sad

    H irresponsible

    J trustworthy

3. "Happy Birthday, Grandpa! Here is your present. I can't wait for you to open it. I chose it just for you. I know you will like it."

    A thoughtful

    B selfish

    C shy

    D happy

4. "Your car needs work. You haven't been taking care of it. It needs an oil change. It's due for a tune-up. The fan belt is loose. The spark plugs need replacing. If you do not take care of your car, it will fall apart. It will cost you more to fix it than to keep it in good working order."

    F helpful and friendly

    G expert but critical

    H lazy and insulting

    J dishonest and hard-working

Practice

Read each paragraph. Think about what the person described in the paragraph is like. Choose the word or phrase from the box that best describes the person. Write the word or phrase on the line.

shy	friendly	selfish
annoying	overly confident	ambitious

1.   Jane never went to the games or dances at school. In the lunchroom, she ate alone. She never sat at a table with anyone else. Most often she kept her eyes on her tray. Sometimes she watched other kids laughing and talking. She wanted to be like them. Yet she couldn't bring herself to talk to anyone.

_____

2.   Greg always has a crowd around him. He's often the center of attention. People like being around him. They listen to and smile at his jokes and stories. Greg seems to be everyone's friend. He enjoys people. As a result, people like him.

_____

3.   Maria has come a long way in ten short years. She started working as a receptionist. Before long, she became an administrative assistant. Then she asked for a sales job. She got it. Soon she was the company's top salesperson. Within two years, she was made sales manager. She always worked hard. She set goals for herself. Her next goal is to become vice president of the company.

_____

4.   Vern worked with many people. He was always correcting them. He pointed out every mistake he thought others made. He corrected people's grammar. He pointed out bad food choices at lunch. He said people did not use office equipment properly. He never had anything good to say about anyone. Everyone avoided Vern. He could not understand why. He was just trying to help them.

_____

Apply

Write a sentence describing what you have learned about each character's personality.

1.   Tonya had worked hard all her life. She did not make much money cleaning houses. Yet she had saved a little money each week. After 30 years of work, she found she had saved a lot of money. "I could retire," she thought, "but what would I do?" Tonya gave some of the money to a charity and kept on working.

    _____

    _____

2.   Tim loves music. He likes all kinds of music. It fills his day. He listens to rap, country, rock 'n' roll, classical, rhythm and blues, and jazz. He likes gospel music as much as he likes show tunes. He enjoys a symphony and a folk song equally. Tim is a program director for a radio station. The station plays all kinds of music. "What would I do," Tim always says, "if there weren't music? Life wouldn't be worth living!"

    _____

    _____

3.   Clarence is a baker. He really enjoys his job. He gets up early every day to make all kinds of breads. He mixes the dough. He shapes the bread dough and bakes it. He likes the smell of baking bread. Most of all, he likes eating hot, fresh bread right out of the oven. So do his many customers who think that his bread is the best in town.

    _____

    _____

4.   Marisa spoke gently to her mother, "Yes, Mama. Is that better, Mama?" She fluffed her mother's pillows. She gave her mother her medicine. She fed her mother. Sometimes Mama was very demanding. Sometimes she spoke sharply to Marisa. Yet Marisa was always patient. She never complained. "Poor Mama," she thought. "Her life has shrunk to the size of a room. I will bring flowers! That will cheer Mama up."

    _____

    _____

Check Up

Circle the answer for each question about character traits.

1. Which of the following would a selfish character do?

   A Give up a seat on the bus to someone.

   B Refuse to share a snack with a friend.

   C Show his or her new car to the neighbors.

   D Laugh at someone else's joke.

2. Which sentence might a confident character say?

   F "I guess I could use some help."

   G "Are you sure we are doing this right?"

   H "I'm sure my project will be the best one in the class."

   J "Maybe we should stop and ask for directions."

3. What might someone say about a friendly person?

   A "You can't trust him, but he's fun to have at a party."

   B "I enjoy his silly jokes. They make me laugh. We've been friends forever."

   C "He still owes me the $50 I loaned him last year. I don't know why I put up with him."

   D "I read that he made a fortune. He'll probably make friends with the rich and famous. We won't see him much now."

4. Which description fits a timid person?

   F He spent hours daydreaming. He saw himself as the strong, silent type.

   G He sunk down in his chair. He covered his face with his paper. He was afraid she would be angry.

   H He saw her coming toward him. He walked to meet her. He would not back down.

   J He always pointed out her errors. He liked knowing he was right and she was wrong.

5. Which sentence might a proud, unbending character say?

   A "Not only do I not need your help, I do not want it!"

   B "I could use a hand, but I hate to bother you."

   C "I've learned to accept all help. I appreciate your offer."

   D "Say, could you help me out here?"

Identifying Character Traits

Writers want you to believe in their characters. They create two kinds of characters. Some characters seem like real people. True-to-life characters are called **dynamic.** Dynamic characters have some good traits. They have some bad traits. They can be strong. Sometimes they are weak. They grow and change through their experiences.

Some characters in stories are **flat**. They show only one trait. They often remain the same throughout the story.

Read about these characters from books, movies, and TV shows. Write *dynamic* or *flat* in the blank to describe each character.

_____ 1. King Midas loved gold more than anything. He could never have enough. One day he was granted a wish. He wished that everything would turn to gold when he touched it.

_____ 2. Luke Skywalker longed to become a fighter pilot. He learned about his own abilities. He grew more confident. Finally, he successfully fought evil forces.

_____ 3. Jo March was a determined young woman. She had once dreamed of becoming an artist. She decided to follow her heart, instead. She and her husband opened a school and home for needy children.

_____ 4. Marge Simpson is the ultimate suburban mom. She keeps peace in the family. She finds the good in everyone. She does all the housework. She cares for the children. She takes care of her husband. She always looks on the bright side.

Practice

Read about each character. Choose the phrase from the box that describes him or her. Write the phrase on the line.

unyielding and stubborn	whiny and dependent
uncertain and indecisive	self-serving and critical

1. George had to control everything. He demanded that things be done his way. He said that only he knew the best way to get things done. He would never compromise. He said that it is either his way or no way.

   _____

2. Helen was always complaining about her boss. She said that he was not good at his job. She always had to complete projects he failed to do. She had made him the success he was. She wanted others to know about all she had done. She wanted credit for what she did. She wanted to be admired.

   _____

3. Martha stopped in the doorway. She frowned. She pouted. She asked in a pleading voice, "Can't you please help me? I can't put up all the decorations myself. You know how much I count on your help. I just can't do anything without you."

   _____

4. Richard does not like to decide anything. I ask him to choose a place to go for dinner. He will not make up his mind. Finally, he just says, "You decide." He doesn't care where we go. Just do not ask him to make the decision. He will not select a movie to see. Anything is fine with him. I choose the movie. I have to decide where and when we should go. Richard just won't or can't make a decision.

   _____

Apply

Read about each character. On the lines, write whether each is *dynamic* or *flat*.
Underline the word or words in the passage that best describe each character.

_____ 1. Roger studies a lot. He knows a lot about math and science and computers. Roger is not popular. Other students play practical jokes on him and laugh at him. He knows he is considered a nerd.

_____ 2. Ruth is a mother and a grandmother. She also is a woman with a secret. Ruth can't read. She has a learning disability. No one discovered it when she was in school. She never told anyone she could not read. Now she is working with a tutor. She is learning to read simple books. She feels excited and proud of her success. She has decided to share her new skill with her family.

_____ 3. Maria Elena's family moved away last spring. Maria Elena spent the whole summer feeling sad. She thought she would never be happy again. School started two weeks ago. At first, Maria Elena disliked the new school. Now, however, she is meeting many people. She is beginning to feel better. She no longer cries herself to sleep at night. She is making new friends. She is learning that change can be good.

_____ 4. Ben is an athlete. He works out at the gym every morning. He practices soccer or tennis every evening. Ben plays on a soccer club team and enters a local tennis competition every year. He thinks of himself as a muscle machine. He spends all of his free time on sports. He doesn't see any limit to his ability.

Check Up

Circle the answer for each question about a character.

1. Which of these is a flat character?

   A someone who grows and changes through the story

   B someone who reveals one trait and does not change

   C someone who has both strengths and weaknesses

   D someone who has both good and bad traits

2. Which of these is a dynamic character?

   F someone who has only good traits

   G someone who is active throughout the story

   H someone who has only bad character traits

   J someone who grows and changes in the story

3. Which of the following is most likely to happen to a true-to-life character?

   A learning patience while caring for a sick relative

   B winning a difficult contest and living happily ever after

   C suddenly changing personality completely after a blow to the head

   D discovering a cure for cancer while tinkering in a high school science lab

4. What is the best word to describe the following character? Mai is afraid to fly. She learns to overcome her fear. Now she enjoys plane trips.

   F flat

   G dynamic

   H weak

   J strong

5. Which of the following is a dynamic character?

   A someone who overcomes shyness and becomes a respected actor

   B someone whose only goal in life is to make money

   C someone who wants adventures but keeps his office job because he needs the money

   D someone who works hard caring for her family and giving little thought to her own needs

6. Why is Wile E. Coyote, a character on the Road Runner cartoons, a flat character?

   F He never wins.

   G He is a cartoon character.

   H He never changes and has only one interest.

   J He appears in every scene in the cartoon.

Recognizing the Main Idea

The **main idea** of a story is the most important idea. It is the point the writer is trying to make about the subject. Details, facts, and examples in a story support the main idea.

The main idea may be stated in a topic sentence. Or, it may not be stated. Sometimes readers must decide what the main idea is by using information in the text.

Underline the sentence in each paragraph that states the main idea.

1. Ben Jonson is one of England's most famous poets and playwrights. He lived in the 17th century. Jonson worked carefully. He often took two years to write a single play. In 1616 he became the first playwright to publish his plays. Publishing the play helped people to see plays as serious works of art. When he died, Jonson was buried in Westminster Abbey in London. Many of England's famous poets are buried there.

2. Many cartoon characters have only four fingers. That includes the thumb. This isn't because they are animal characters. Human characters often have only four fingers, too. In cartoons, four fingers look better than five. It's hard to draw five fingers on one hand and make them look real. Cartoon characters are small, and so are their hands. A fifth finger makes the hands look too big. So cartoonists just leave off one finger.

3. Of all birds, the best hunter is the golden eagle. It has a number of useful features for hunting. It has a wingspan of up to seven feet. Its wide wings help the eagle fly fast. It has talons, or claws, that are strong. The eagle has sharp eyesight. It can easily spot prey. Very few animals can escape its attack. The bird swoops in with great speed. It grabs the animal. Then it carries its catch away.

4. Arthur L. Nalls built and rode a very small bicycle. His bicycle was just five inches high! It was the smallest bicycle anyone ever rode. The bike was very strong. It had to be to support a full-grown person. Nalls built the bike at the United States Naval Academy. Many TV viewers saw him ride the bike.

Practice

Read each passage. Then circle the sentence that states the main idea.

1. Many people fly their country's flag on holidays. Most people want to show respect for their flags and their countries. They know that there are special ways to take care of flags. Yet many people do not know how to care for the flags. For example, flags can become dull and dirty. Some people do not wash them. They think it is disrespectful to get them wet. This isn't true. Most official flags are washed regularly. Keeping a flag clean shows respect for the flag and the country.

    A Dirty flags should be washed.

    B Some people think it is not respectful to wash flags.

    C There are ways to take care of flags to show respect for them.

2. Crocodiles will eat most kinds of birds. They do not eat one kind of bird, however. It's a bird called the zic-zac. The zic-zac gets and gives special treatment. When a crocodile comes ashore, it opens its mouth. The zic-zac climbs inside without fear. It eats the leeches that have attached themselves inside the crocodile's mouth. The zic-zac gets a good meal. The crocodile gets a clean mouth.

    F Animals have various ways of helping each other.

    G The zic-zac and the crocodile help one another.

    H Zic-zacs enjoy eating leeches.

3. Stained glass windows can be found in many churches. People expect to see them there. Yet, one of the most famous stained glass windows is in a New York airport. The stained-glass window in New York's Kennedy Airport is the largest one in the world. It is made up of many small pieces of colored glass. Each piece is held in place by lead solder.

    A Stained glass is made up of many small pieces of colored glass.

    B Stained glass can be found in buildings other than churches.

    C The largest stained glass window can be seen at New York's Kennedy Airport.

Apply

Read each passage. Then write a sentence that tells its main idea.

1.   In 1974 some people in Little Rock, Arkansas, baked a large pizza. At the time, it was the largest pizza ever made. This pizza used lots of fresh ingredients. Hundreds of pounds of tomatoes and cheese went into it. In fact, the whole thing weighed 1,200 pounds! The finished pizza was 25 feet across. It was baked in the ovens of the Pizza Inn. Many people feasted on it at the restaurant. It was too big to be moved.

_____

_____

2.   A medina is a kind of shopping center. It is a Tunisian market. Tunisia is a country in northern Africa. A medina has stores arranged by what they sell. Stores that sell the same kinds of things are grouped together. Each type of product is on a different street. This means that the stores compete for the same customers. Buyers can get good prices. However, they may have to walk a lot when they want to buy different products.

_____

_____

3.   When your foot "falls sleep," it's not because it is tired. You might have had it bent the wrong way. You may have been sitting on it for a while. A foot falls asleep when it doesn't get enough blood. Blood flows to the foot through blood vessels in the leg. As it flows, it washes wastes out of the limbs. When you sit on your foot or bend it sharply, you block off the blood vessels. Blood can't flow freely and carry away the wastes. The wastes collect and block nerve endings. Nerves then can't carry messages to the brain. So you can't feel your foot. The "pins and needles" you feel as your foot wakes up are the nerves going back to work.

_____

_____

Check Up

Read the passage. Then circle the answer for each question.

Most frozen food has been treated to kill the germs that would cause it to spoil. Food that has been thawed and exposed to air is likely to spoil. Freezing food that has been exposed to air and germs will not kill those germs. It will only slow their growth. That's why food experts say that you should never refreeze food that has thawed. Thawed food should be cooked and eaten soon, so it won't spoil and cause food poisoning.

1. What is the passage about?

   A the danger of food poisoning

   B selecting a good freezer

   C the danger of refreezing thawed food

   D how germs cause food to spoil

2. Which of the following details would fit this paragraph?

   F how people catch colds

   G why some children are spoiled

   H how to keep germs out of thawing food

   J why you should cook pork well

3. Which sentence best states the main idea of the paragraph?

   A Frozen food that has thawed should not be refrozen.

   B Most frozen food has been treated to kill germs.

   C Eat only fresh foods because frozen foods contain germs.

   D Germs are everywhere, and they cause food to spoil.

4. Which sentence does not support the main idea in the paragraph?

   F Most frozen food has been treated to kill the germs that would cause it to spoil.

   G Food that has been thawed and exposed to air is likely to spoil.

   H Freezing food that has been exposed to air and germs will not kill those germs.

   J People have a lot of germs on their hands when they handle food.

5. What does a main idea sentence do?

   A It contains a new idea.

   B It supports the main idea.

   C It states the paragraph's most important idea.

   D It has many details.

Identifying the Main Idea

The **main idea** of a paragraph is often stated in a **topic sentence**. A topic sentence tells the point the writer is making. Other sentences in the paragraph give details, facts, and examples about the main idea.

Underline the sentence that states the main idea for each of the following paragraphs.

1. Whales live in the ocean. Yet, they are not fish. Whales are mammals that come to the surface to breathe. When they are underwater, they must hold their breath. Some whales must breathe every 5 to 10 minutes. Other species can remain underwater for up to an hour. As a whale holds its breath, the air in its lungs becomes warm and moist. When the whale finally surfaces, it blows this air out through the blowhole in the top of its head. It also draws fresh air in through its blowhole.

2. Sometimes zoo animals need to get away from people. Lions, seals, and pandas do not like noisy crowds. The crowds can make them nervous. Sometimes they go to a quiet spot. They try to get away from people. The keepers of the Tokyo Zoo know that the animals need a rest. They shut down the zoo for two months every year. This helps the animals relax and rest.

3. Minerals in hair may show how smart a person is. It seems the secret of intelligence is seen in each strand of hair. Hair contains many minerals. Two of them are copper and zinc. A study shows that a high amount of zinc or copper in hair may be a sign of intelligence.

4. Today the lion is often called the king of the beasts. The original king of beasts, however, was *Tyrannosaurus rex,* a huge meat-eating dinosaur. This name means "king of the tyrant lizards." Tyrannosaurus was a huge dinosaur. It was twice as large as an elephant. Its head was more than four feet long. It had sharp teeth and claws. It was a meateater and hunted for prey. Experts say it could run fast despite its size. Like all dinosaurs, tyrannosaurus is now extinct.

Practice

Read each paragraph. Underline the topic sentence. Then circle the sentence that restates the main idea.

1. Many chemicals make up the human body. They combine to make the cells of the body. Cells are made up of water, protein, fat, sugar, and starch. These are all chemical compounds. Most of these compounds contain hydrogen, oxygen, and carbon. Proteins also contain nitrogen. All cells have salts, vitamins, and enzymes. These are also made of combinations of chemicals. Some cells have a lot of one type of chemical. For instance, red blood cells have lots of iron. Bone cells have lots of calcium. Oxygen makes up 65 percent of the human body.

   A The human body is complicated.

   B The human body is 65 percent oxygen.

   C The human body is made up of many different chemicals.

2. Why does a newborn want to hold your hand? Put your finger in a newborn baby's hand and see what happens. The baby will try to grab it tightly. This grasping urge is a reflex. Humans share this grasping reflex with monkeys. A reflex is something an animal does without thinking. A young monkey spends a lot of time riding on its mother's back. To stay on, it has to hold on tightly.

   F Monkeys and humans have some things in common.

   G Baby monkeys and humans both have the grasping reflex.

   H Babies grab things and hold on tightly.

3. Alfred Hitchcock has been called the master of suspense films. He directed many classic movies. These include *Psycho, The Birds*, and *Dial M for Murder*. These movies kept audiences on the edges of their seats. Hitchcock planned his films very carefully. He thought out every shot in detail long before the cameras rolled. It was said that Hitchcock did most of his movie-making in his head, not through a camera.

   A Alfred Hitchcock was a master at making suspense films.

   B Alfred Hitchcock was extremely good at his job.

   C Alfred Hitchcock planned his movies well before they were filmed.

Apply

Read each list of details for each paragraph. Then write a topic sentence for the paragraph. Check your sentence. Do all the details relate to its point?

1. Details:
   California condors are disappearing because of people.
   People have used up much of the forest land where condors need to live.
   Poisons used by farmers also killed some of these giant birds.
   Not many baby condors are born each year.
   Laws protect them, but people fear the condors will soon all be gone.

   Topic Sentence:

   _____

   _____

2. Details:
   Rattlesnakes are among the slowest-moving snakes.
   Their venom can kill, but people can easily avoid being bitten.
   Rattlesnakes bite only in self-defense.
   Their venomous bite protects them.

   Topic Sentence:

   _____

   _____

3. Details:
   People in Santa Rosa planned to build a footbridge.
   But people couldn't agree on the plan and the cost.
   They kept arguing about it.
   Tony Asaro and Jeff Cole were two teens living in Santa Rosa.
   While the arguing continued, the boys built the footbridge themselves.

   Topic Sentence:

   _____

   _____

Check Up

Read the paragraph. Then circle the answer for each item.

Cover your mouth when you sneeze! That's what most children are taught. In fact, most people try to hold back the rush of air when they sneeze. It's the polite thing to do, but it's not the safe thing to do. A sneeze means the body is trying to force something harmful out. If you have a cold, your body is trying to force germs out through the nose. In a sneeze, air leaves the nose with great speed and force. That's why it's dangerous to hold a sneeze in. The air will be forced out into the sinuses and ears. The germs can infect the eardrums. It's true that sneezing can spread germs to other people. Even covering your nose with a handkerchief can't stop that. Germs are so tiny that they go through the cloth.

1. Tell why the following sentence is **not** the main idea of the paragraph: *Holding a sneeze in can damage the eardrums.*

   A It is too general.

   B It is too narrow. It only tells part of what the passage is about.

   C It does not stick to the main point.

   D It contains false information.

2. Tell why the following sentence is **not** the main idea of the paragraph: *Sneezing is a sudden and violent rush of air out through the nose and mouth.*

   F It is too general.

   G It is too narrow. It only tells part of what the passage is about.

   H It does not stick to the main point.

   J It contains false information.

3. Tell why the following sentence is a good main idea for the paragraph: *Holding in a sneeze is polite, but it's not good for the body.*

   A It introduces a new topic.

   B It gives a complete definition.

   C It summarizes the points made about sneezing.

   D It does not include all the supporting details.

Read On   Look for the main idea as you read "Coretta Scott King: The Dream Lives On." Then answer the questions.

Comparing and Contrasting

Writers often **compare** things. They tell how the things are alike. They **contrast** things, too. They tell how things are different. Writers sometimes give clues to let readers know whether they are making comparisons or contrasts. The words listed below are some of the clue words writers use.

Words That Show Comparison
and	both	like	similarly
as	likewise	in the same way	

Words That Show Contrast
although	however	unlike	still
but	in contrast	on the other hand	

Write *comparison* if the sentence shows how two things are alike. Write *contrast* if it shows how they are different. Underline the clue words that signal comparison or contrast.

_____ 1. The day was sunny but cooler than expected.

_____ 2. Fish use gills to take oxygen from water; however, whales must breathe air.

_____ 3. Like her sister, Regina had quite a temper.

_____ 4. Both President Lincoln and President Kennedy were assassinated.

_____ 5. Isaac plays the piano as well as he plays the guitar.

_____ 6. I'd like to go out tonight; on the other hand, there's a program on TV I want to watch.

_____ 7. A butterfly has slender antennae; in contrast, a moth's antennae are thick.

_____ 8. Unlike air travel, traveling by train offers scenic views of the countryside.

_____ 9. Wolves in a pack have a pecking order with one wolf accepted as the leader; similarly, your dog accepts you as "boss."

_____ 10. Nick refused to budge in the same way that a stubborn mule digs in its hooves and pulls back.

Practice

Fill in the blanks with clue words that signal a comparison. Choose clue words from the list below.

and	both	like	similarly
as	likewise	in the same way	

1. The Grand Canyon is a popular tourist attraction _____ is Yellowstone.

2. _____ limes _____ lemons are citrus fruits.

3. An iris grows from a bulb _____ a tulip does.

4. A wild cat spends much time alone; _____, house cats are independent.

Fill in the blanks with clue words that signal a contrast. Choose clue words from the list below.

although	however	unlike	still
but	in contrast	on the other hand	

5. _____ the quiet dawn, the sunset was rich with color.

6. _____ the day had begun badly, it turned out to be my lucky day.

7. Many successful people have a college degree; _____, many people have succeeded without one.

8. John loves designer clothes; _____, he can't afford to buy them.

Apply

For each pair of words, write a sentence making a comparison. Use clue words that signal a comparison. Then write a sentence making a contrast. Use clue words that signal a contrast.

1. broccoli and cauliflower

    _____

    _____

2. Independence Day and Memorial Day

    _____

    _____

3. a rose and a daisy

    _____

    _____

4. a ballpoint pen and a pencil

    _____

    _____

5. a hurricane and a tornado

    _____

    _____

6. parents and grandparents

    _____

    _____

Check Up

Read the paragraph. Then circle the answer for each question.

You are a mammal just as a dog, cat, whale, and monkey are mammals. Like all mammals, you have hair and your internal body temperature remains constant. All female mammals have mammary glands that give milk to feed young. What sets you apart? Unlike most mammals, people have hands that can grasp. They also have a brain that can think and reason. Monkeys and apes also do these things, but they do not use their abilities together in the same way people do. Only humans put brain and hand together to make cities and computers and words. Unlike other mammals, you use written language.

1. What two things are compared and contrasted in this paragraph?

    A people and dogs

    B monkeys and apes

    C humans and other mammals

    D you and all other animals

2. Which of the following is a way that people are like all mammals?

    F Females have mammary glands and feed milk to offspring.

    G People walk on two feet.

    H People can think and reason.

    J People have hands that can grasp.

3. Which of the following is a way in which people are different from other mammals?

    A People can think and reason.

    B People have a constant body temperature.

    C People create by using brain and hand together.

    D People communicate with each other.

4. In the second sentence of the paragraph, what word signals that a comparison will be made?

    F you

    G all

    H like

    J constant

5. Which word signals that a contrast will be made?

    A and

    B also

    C like

    D but

6. The last sentence in the paragraph shows a contrast because

    F it describes how people are like other mammals

    G it describes how people are unlike other mammals

    H it is the opposite of the first sentence

    J it is the same as the first sentence

Using Comparison and Contrast

When you **compare and contrast** two things, you show how they are alike and how they are different.

First look at ways the things are alike. Then look for ways they are different. A table like this can help you get organized.

	How They Are Alike	How They Are Different
Apples and Oranges	• fruits, grow on trees	• apples have cores; oranges don't • oranges are orange; apples are red or green or yellow

Read the details about Venus and Earth. Write details that show how the planets are alike in the first column. Write details that show how they are different in the second column.

Earth and Venus are about the same size. Earth has much life and water. Venus is too hot for life to develop. Venus is the planet closest to Earth. Venus has thick clouds. Earth has an atmosphere with clouds. Earth's atmosphere contains oxygen. Venus's atmosphere has sulfuric acid. Earth and Venus have about the same mass and density.

Earth and Venus

Alike	Different

Practice

For each pair, circle the details that tell how they are alike. Underline details that show how they are different.

1. cats and dogs

   four legs   related to wolves

   fur covered   ability to climb trees

2. grass and dandelion

   has a yellow bloom   has a smooth, simple leaf

   has spreading roots   is a green plant

3. gloves and mittens

   their uses   materials used to make them

   their shapes   how they cover the fingers

4. goldfish and shark

   size   lives in water

   color   breathes with gills

5. ladder and stairs

   is movable   situations in which it is used

   has equally spaced steps   way of moving up or down

6. a poem and a song

   rhythm   set to music

   rhyme   stanzas

Apply

For each set of information, write two sentences. In one, tell one way the things are alike. In the other, tell one way the things are different. Use clue words that show that things are alike or different.

1. *The Rocky Mountains:* in North America; tall, sharp peaks; ice-capped; younger mountains; rise far above surrounding land
   The Appalachian Mountains: in North America; gently rounded peaks; shorter, worn down by time and erosion; very ancient; rise far above surrounding land

   _____

   _____

2. *a housefly:* insect; six legs; wings; lives independently
   an ant: insect; six legs; no wings; lives in organized communities

   _____

   _____

3. *a dance class:* all move through same steps together; move to music; learn steps to dance for pleasure
   an aerobics class: all move through same steps together; move to music; keep moving to get fit

   _____

   _____

4. *a fork:* eating tool; four or five narrow, sharp tines at end to spear food; flat handle fits hand
   a spoon: eating tool; small, shallow bowl at end to lift, stir, or measure food; flat handle fits hand

   _____

   _____

Check Up

Read the paragraph. Then circle the answer for each question.

Have you heard of the dodo and the blue pigeon? These two birds no longer exist. Both lived on Mauritius Island. They could not be found anywhere else. In many ways, the birds were quite different. The dodo was clumsy. It could not fly. The blue pigeon flew gracefully. The dodo nested on the ground. The blue pigeon nested in trees. You might think these differences would protect the blue pigeon more than the dodo. However, these pigeons became extinct, just as the dodo did. The pigeons were delicious. People shot them for food and sport.

1. What is the purpose of this paragraph?

   A to describe the dodo and the blue pigeon

   B to compare and contrast the dodo and the blue pigeon

   C to show how the dodo and the blue pigeon are alike

   D to show how the dodo and the blue pigeon are different

2. What is one way the two birds were alike?

   F ability to fly

   G nesting habits

   H clumsiness

   J lived only on Mauritius Island

3. What is one way the two birds were different?

   A killed off by humans

   B extinction

   C nesting habits

   D location

4. Which sentences in the paragraph show contrasts?

   F The dodo nested on the ground. The blue pigeon nested in trees.

   G The blue pigeon flew gracefully. The dodo nested on the ground.

   H The pigeons were delicious. People shot them for food and sport.

   J Have you heard of the dodo and the blue pigeon? These two birds no longer exist.

5. Which sentences in the paragraph compare similarities?

   A In many ways, the birds were quite different. The dodo was clumsy.

   B These two birds no longer exist. Both lived on Mauritius Island.

   C The dodo was clumsy. It could not fly.

   D The dodo nested on the ground. The blue pigeon nested in trees.

Drawing Conclusions

Drawing a conclusion is making a judgment based on facts and what experience has taught you. The facts "add up." They lead you to understand the writer's point. To draw conclusions from what you read, pay close attention.

Choose the conclusion from the box that fits each passage and write it on the lines.

> Without sunlight, plants would die, and without food, animals would die.
>
> Therefore, rocks are not living things.
>
> Since a wooden chair is made from a tree that was once alive, it has cells.
>
> Robots are not living.

1. All living things are made up of cells. Robots are not made up of cells.

    _____

    _____

2. A cell is the basic unit of a living thing. It performs all the processes needed to live. Cells are found in nonliving matter only when that matter once was alive and now is dead.

    _____

    _____

3. Living things need energy to live. Plants get energy from sunlight. Animals and people get energy from the food they eat.

    _____

    _____

4. Living things grow and change. The growth and change must come from within the thing. Although objects like rocks change over time, the change is brought about by outside forces.

    _____

    _____

Practice

Read each paragraph. Circle the conclusion that can be drawn from the facts.

1.   Ibexes are wild mountain goats. They live in the Alps. They also live in the mountains of Asia. They climb slopes that are nearly straight up and down. They jump from rock to rock. They leap across gaps as wide as 40 feet.

From these facts, you can conclude that

A ibexes are clumsy and stupid

B ibexes do not understand how high up they are

C ibexes are adapted to live in mountains

2.   Long ago, some people made clothes from tree bark. Africans did so about five thousand years ago. Long ago, some American Indians also made clothes from bark. Both people made the clothes in the same way. They soaked the bark in water. They put wet strips of bark together. They pounded the strips with stones. The pounding caused fibers to shake out of the bark and stick together. Once dry, the fibers were ready to be shaped into clothing.

From these facts, you can conclude that

A the Africans taught the American Indians to make bark cloth

B American Indians came from Africa

C American Indians and Africans came up with the same way of working with the same material

3.   The Gila (he´-luh) monster lives in deserts of Mexico and the Southwestern United States. It is one of only two lizards that are venomous. When it bites, it locks its jaws just as bulldogs do. The Gila monster hangs on, though. It holds on tight and injects its venom.

From these facts, you can conclude that

A Gila monsters are related to the other venomous lizard

B some desert animals fear the Gila monster

C Gila monsters never attack people

Apply

Read each passage. On the lines, write the conclusion you can draw from the facts.

1.   Birds are built to fly. They have lightweight bones. They use large amounts of energy, just as airplanes do. Their bodies release the energy stored in food quickly and efficiently. This helps them stay lightweight. Birds' have powerful flight muscles attached to a large breastbone. They have strong, light feathers. These feathers have many rows of barbs that lock together to make them strong and firm.

    From these facts, I can conclude that

    _____

    _____

2.   Birds do not know how to fly at birth, even though flying is natural for them. As it grows, a baby bird becomes restless. It starts stretching its wings. It walks around the nest and tests its wings. The parent bird helps the baby get strong by holding food at a distance. The baby bird must struggle across the nest to get it. One day, the baby hops over the edge of the nest with its wings unfurled. The parents fly off the branch. The baby follows, flapping its wings furiously. The young bird's skill quickly improves.

    From these facts, I can conclude that

    _____

    _____

3.   Birds do not have to flap their wings constantly to remain in the air. If they did, they would soon be worn out. Instead, the shape of their wings provides lift. The upper surface of the wing is rounded. Air has farther to go over than under the wing. Air above the wing moves faster; this difference creates a higher air pressure under the wing. This is called lift. The larger the wing, the greater the lift. Some big birds soar and glide for a long time without flapping their wings.

    From these facts, I can conclude that

    _____

    _____

Check Up

Read the passage. Then circle the response that completes each statement.

An igloo is an Inuit snow house. It is strong, weatherproof, and can be built quickly. First, a trench is cut in the snow. Blocks are cut from the walls of the trench. Each block is shaped to lean inward when set in place. The blocks are laid in circular rows, one on top of another. Each ring grows smaller around. At last, a one-block hole is left at the top. A wedge-shaped block is set into the top hole. Next, the builder fills cracks with soft snow. Then a lighted lamp is placed inside. As the snow begins to melt, the blocks become saturated with water. Then the lamp is put out and cold air is allowed in. The igloo is soon transformed into a dome of ice.

1. From the description of the ice blocks and their placement, you could conclude that

   A the blocks get larger as the igloo goes up

   B the blocks are perfectly square

   C the igloo is not straight or stable

   D the igloo's shape is half a sphere

2. From the last four sentences of the passage, you could conclude that

   F the builder is not careful with the lamp

   G the ice shell inside the igloo makes it weatherproof

   H Inuits would soon freeze in an igloo

   J the snow is melted to make the igloo larger inside

3. From the entire passage, you could conclude that

   A igloos are dangerous to build

   B igloos are large enough for only two people

   C igloos are carefully engineered

   D igloos are the best designed houses in the world

4. You could not conclude how many people can live in an igloo because

   F the passage does not discuss its size

   G the passage does not tell you how many people are needed to build an igloo

   H only one person builds the igloo

   J the passage gives several possible answers

More Drawing Conclusions

Here is a formula for **drawing a conclusion**:

General statement	+	**Specific example**	=	**Conclusion**
All animals need water.		Camels are animals.		Camels need water.

The general statement and the example must be true. If they are, then the conclusion is true. If either one is not true, then the conclusion is not true. The example must fit the general statement. For example, if the example above said, "Trees are animals," the conclusion would be false because trees are not animals.

Read each argument. Circle any statement that is not true. Write _true_ or _false_ on the line before the argument.

_____ **1.** All people need oxygen to live.
You are a human being.
You need oxygen.

_____ **2.** All sparrows have feathers.
A mouse is a sparrow.
A mouse has feathers.

_____ **3.** All people breathe.
Our cat Rags breathes.
Rags is a person.

_____ **4.** All people eat.
Peggy is a person.
Peggy eats.

_____ **5.** All two-legged animals are human.
An ostrich has two legs.
An ostrich is human.

_____ **6.** All big, heavy vehicles use a lot of gas.
A truck is a big, heavy vehicle.
A truck uses a lot of gas.

Practice

Read each pair of true statements. Choose the conclusion you can make from each pair.

1. All butterflies are insects.
   A monarch is a butterfly.

   A A monarch is an insect.   **B** Every insect is a butterfly.

2. All people eat food.
   Joe is a person.

   A Joe exercises.   **B** Joe eats food.

3. All insects have six legs.
   A spider has eight legs.

   A A spider must be an insect.   **B** A spider cannot be an insect.

4. All plants make their own food.
   An oak tree is a plant.

   A An oak tree makes its own food.   **B** An oak tree has large roots.

5. Every homeowner in town must pay real estate tax.
   The Smiths own a home in town.

   A The Smiths pay real estate tax.   **B** The Smiths must sell their home.

6. Every four years a presidential election is held.
   It has been four years since the last election.

   A Next year there will be an election.   **B** This year there will be an election.

7. Paul always bakes cookies during the holidays.
   The holidays are next week.

   A Paul will go on vacation next week.   **B** Paul will bake cookies next week.

8. All the seniors have paid for their graduation robes.
   Rhaki is a senior.

   A Rhaki will graduate.   **B** Rhaki has paid for her graduation robe.

Apply

Read each general statement and specific example. Write a conclusion based on the pair of sentences.

1. All dogs are descended from wild ancestors.
   The collie is a dog.

   _____

2. Only female mosquitoes feed on blood.
   A mosquito just bit me.

   _____

3. All rodents gnaw on hard things to wear down their teeth.
   A rabbit is a rodent.

   _____

4. All English words have the same number of syllables as they have vowel sounds.
   The word *chrysanthemum* has four vowel sounds.

   _____

Read each set of sentences. The boldfaced sentence contains a mistake. Cross it out and rewrite the sentence correctly so that the conclusion is true.

5. **Only dogs purr.**

   _____

   My pet is purring.
   My pet must be a cat.

6. **All cats have hooves.**

   _____

   Triple Play is a horse.
   Triple Play has hooves.

Check Up

Read each set of sentences. Then circle the response that answers each question or completes each statement.

Sentences

A All proper adjectives begin with a capital letter.

B The word *English* is a proper adjective.

C The word *English* should begin with a capital letter.

1. Sentence C is true because

   A A is true, but B is false

   B B is true, but A is false

   C A and B are true

   D neither A nor B is true

2. Which sentence makes a general statement that is true?

   F sentence A

   G sentence B

   H sentence C

   J none of the sentences

3. Which sentence is a specific example of the general statement?

   A sentence A

   B sentence B

   C sentence C

   D none of the sentences

4. Which sentence is the conclusion you can draw logically from the other two?

   F sentence A

   G sentence B

   H sentence C

   J none of the sentences

Sentences

A All reptiles are cold-blooded.

B A cat is a reptile.

C Cats are cold-blooded.

5. Why is sentence C not true?

   A because sentence A is not true

   B because sentence B is not true

   C because sentences A and B are not true

   D because it doesn't use the same words as A and B

Read On As you read "What We Know About Memory," look for conclusions. Then answer the questions.

Recognizing Cause and Effect

Writers use **cause and effect** to explain how events affect one another. Try the "because" test. If you can use the word *because* to show that two events or facts are related, then they have a cause-and-effect relationship.

Cause and effect signal words include the following:

as a result	due to	so
because	if, then	therefore
consequently	since	thus

Add *because* between the sentences. Write *yes* if the relationship is cause and effect. Write *no* if it is not.

_____ 1. Our water supply is polluted _____ factories pour wastes into the rivers and lakes.

_____ 2. The buffalo nearly became extinct _____ people killed thousands of them for sport.

_____ 3. Charles lost the election _____ it rained on election day.

_____ 4. There was a total eclipse of the moon _____ it was cloudy.

Underline the word or words that signal a cause-and-effect relationship in each sentence. Circle the effect.

5. Since scooters have once again become popular, injuries from scooter accidents have risen.

6. I got a C on my last exam; therefore, I now have a B average in science.

7. Because the bus broke down, we were late for our first class.

8. A big discount store opened outside town; as a result, several small shops downtown lost business and failed.

Practice

Write a word or phrase from the list to make each sentence show cause and effect. Underline the effect.

as a result	due to	so that
because	if/then	therefore
consequently	since	thus

1. I stopped exercising; _____, I have gained weight.

2. _____ I forgot my key, I could not get into the house.

3. _____ you do not enter the contest, _____ you cannot win it.

4. I got my hair cut _____ I would not have to fuss with it constantly.

5. That author's books always sell well; _____, she earns a lot of money.

6. Juney has to follow a strict diet _____ she is diabetic.

7. The ducklings followed me everywhere _____ they thought I was their mother.

8. We fertilized the yard heavily this spring; _____, our grass is thick and green.

9. _____ you give us a 10 percent deposit, _____ we will hold the house for you.

10. Farmers have not finished planting their crops _____ the heavy rains of the past month.

Apply

Read each pair of sentences. Use the term in parentheses to connect them and show a cause-and-effect relationship. Remember to change capitalization and punctuation when you combine both sentences.

1. I dropped the phone. I can't get a dial tone. (because)

   _____

2. Megan slipped and fell on a concrete floor. She broke her wrist. (as a result)

   _____

3. It rains more than six inches in a day. The river will rise and flood the town. (if/then)

   _____

4. Interest rates rose dramatically. Sales of homes fell. (consequently)

   _____

5. Health care has improved. More people are living longer. (because)

   _____

6. American families move more often now than in the past. Children must change schools more often. (as a result)

   _____

7. The cost of living has skyrocketed. Most families need two wage earners. (since)

   _____

8. The dog's tail hit the vase. The vase fell and broke. (so)

   _____

Check Up

Circle the answer for each question.

1. What is a cause in this sentence?

   Because they felt their economy and way of life were threatened, the Southerners went to war against the Union and the Civil War began.

   A Southerners went to war.

   B The Civil War began.

   C Southerners felt their way of life was threatened.

   D Southern economy was ruined.

2. What is the effect in this sentence?

   General Lee surrendered because he realized the South could not win the Civil War.

   F Lee surrendered.

   G Lee knew the South could not win.

   H Lee commanded the Confederate army.

   J Lee defeated the South.

3. Which word or phrase should be used in the blank to show cause and effect?

   During the Civil War, medical care for soldiers was poor; _____, many wounded soldiers died.

   A if

   B because

   C since

   D as a result

4. Which word should be used in the blank to show cause and effect?

   _____ all shipping and transportation had been cut off, the South's economy was destroyed by the end of the Civil War.

   F Therefore

   G Since

   H So

   J Thus

Identifying Cause and Effect

A cause may have more than one effect.

Cause: The world population doubles in size.

Effects: Countries are overcrowded.
Food is in short supply.
Diseases spread easily.

An effect may result from several causes.

Causes: Elephants are hunted for their tusks.
They reproduce slowly.
Their habitats are destroyed.

Effect: Elephants are in danger of becoming extinct.

Read each list of events. Circle each cause. Draw a box around each effect.

1. Brian's job didn't pay well.

   Brian didn't like his boss.

   Brian didn't like his job.

   Brian quit his job.

2. A rash of burglaries hit the city.

   People became nervous.

   The police worked overtime.

   The mayor promised a speedy solution to the problem.

Practice

Study each set of events. Then list the causes and the effects.

1. The days grew short. The weather turned colder. The geese flew south.

   Causes: _____

   _____

   Effect: _____

2. The furnace stopped working. The pipes in the house froze. The houseplants died.

   Cause: _____

   Effects: _____

   _____

3. Heavy rain flooded the town. Houses were destroyed. Drinking water was scarce. People were evacuated.

   Cause: _____

   Effects: _____

   _____

   _____

Apply

Write the missing cause or effect in each column.

1. Causes

The male bird sings a song to attract the female bird.

The male bird fights other males for the female.

The male bird does a dance to attract the female bird.

Effect

_____

_____

2. Cause

_____

_____

Effects

Students pour from classes into the halls.

Lockers clang noisily.

Students with backpacks head for buses.

3. Causes

You eat plenty of fruits, vegetables, and whole grains.

You rest well eight hours a night.

You exercise regularly.

Effect

_____

_____

Check Up

Circle the answer for each question.

1. Which of the following caused the other events to happen?

   A I was late for school.

   B I missed the bus.

   C I overslept this morning.

   D I had to skip breakfast.

2. Which of the following was caused by the other events?

   F Traffic was heavy and slow.

   G Sunlight was glaring off the windshields.

   H I had a roaring headache by the time I reached work.

   J Exhaust fumes filled the air.

3. Which of the following caused the other events to happen?

   A I was determined to buy the red truck.

   B I saved half my paycheck every week.

   C I asked for cash for my birthday.

   D I quit spending money on junk food, games, and CDs.

4. Which of the following was caused by the other events?

   F At last, the puppy was housebroken.

   G I let the puppy out every hour.

   H I praised the puppy every time it went outside.

   J I scolded the puppy when it had accidents in the house.

5. Which of the following caused the other events to happen?

   A I checked interesting cookbooks out of the library.

   B I watched Mama closely when she cooked my favorite dishes.

   C I began making simple meals when Mama could supervise.

   D I decided it was time for me to learn to cook.

6. Which of the following was caused by the other events?

   F Asian beetles attacked the tree.

   G Woodpeckers pecked many holes in the tree.

   H Lightning struck the tree.

   J The weakened tree died.

Summarizing and Paraphrasing

In a **summary**, you use your own words to give the main ideas of a passage. You do not include a lot of detail.

In a **paraphrase**, you restate something in your own words. You include details.

Read each passage. Decide whether the rewritings below it are summaries or paraphrases. Circle the word *summary* or *paraphrase* to show your choice.

1. If you live next to a dog pound, you won't get much sleep. The dogs bark a lot. But you could live next to 100,000 rabbits and never hear them. Scientists once thought that rabbits didn't have voices. By voices they meant the ability to make sounds. Closer study has shown, however, that all warm-blooded creatures, including the rabbit, have voices.

    Summary   **Paraphrase**

    Dogs make plenty of noise when they bark. But rabbits seem to have no voice. Scientists have found that every warm-blooded animal does have the ability to utter sounds.

    Summary   **Paraphrase**

    Although they seem silent, rabbits do have voices. All warm-blooded animals, scientists have learned, can "talk."

2. People do a great deal of walking in their lifetimes. Many people would be amazed to find out how many miles they have walked. Most people walk a distance that would add up to a trip around the world. Experts say that most 80-year-olds have taken enough steps to have walked six times around the world.

    Summary   **Paraphrase**

    The distance a person walks in a lifetime adds up to an amazing amount. It equals from one to six trips around the world.

    Summary   **Paraphrase**

    Over their whole lives, people walk a lot. It surprises most of us to learn we have walked so many miles. It could add up to a trip around the world. In 80 years of steps, a person would have walked enough to add up to six trips around the world.

Practice

Read the passages. Then circle the statement that best summarizes each passage.

1. In Japan, a two-room home can be turned into four rooms in just a few minutes. Many Japanese homes have movable walls. They are not like walls that Americans are used to. Instead of using plaster walls, the Japanese use screens to divide rooms. These screens are lightweight and easy to move. As a result, the house can be changed to fit almost any occasion.

    A Japanese homes are different from other homes because of their small size and moving parts.

    B Japanese homes are generally only two rooms.

    C The Japanese use lightweight screens as walls, making it easy to change space.

    D Americans use plaster for walls while the Japanese use lightweight, easy-to-move screens.

2. Paprika is a spice. It is bright red and is usually ground into a powder. Some people think that paprika has no flavor. They think it is used only to add color to food. But paprika does have a mild flavor. It is warm and slightly sweet. Paprika also has vitamins. It contains vitamins A and C. In fact, there is more vitamin C in paprika than in citrus fruits. But people eat paprika in smaller amounts than they eat oranges or grapefruit.

    F Because paprika has no flavor, it is used in food mostly for its color.

    G Paprika is a spice useful for adding color, mild flavor, and vitamins A and C to foods.

    H Paprika is a better source of vitamins than oranges or grapefruit.

    J Paprika is a spice that is bright red and is powdered.

Apply

Read the passage. Then write a paraphrase of it. Remember to use your own words. Then write a summary of the passage. The summary should be no more than two sentences.

Inside each of your ears is a tiny, thin flap of skin. It is your eardrum. Behind the eardrum are three tiny bones. They are connected to a canal full of fluid. When sound waves hit your ear, they make your eardrum vibrate. This drumming, in turn, sets the three tiny bones in motion. Finally, all this motion causes the fluid in the canal to vibrate. This stimulates nearby nerve cells that are connected to the brain. What the ear does is translate sound into vibration. The vibrations are then changed into nerve impulses. The impulses give a message to the brain.

Paraphrase

_____

_____

_____

_____

_____

_____

_____

_____

Summary

_____

_____

_____

_____

_____

Check Up

Circle the response that answers each question or completes each statement.

1. Sailors have always believed that dolphins bring good luck and should not be harmed.

   Which of the following is a good paraphrase for this sentence?

   A If dolphins swim around a ship at sea, it will have good luck on its voyage.

   B Some creatures are considered lucky.

   C Sailors protect dolphins because they believe dolphins bring good luck.

   D People believe dolphins are able to predict the weather.

2. Some old jobs have been given new job titles. Ministers are clergy, not clergymen. Firemen are firefighters. Why were the names changed? Many of these jobs are now filled by women. They were once held only by men.

   Which of the following is a good summary for this paragraph?

   F Some job titles are changing because women as well as men hold the jobs.

   G Women now hold jobs that were once held only by men.

   H Clergy and firefighters may be either men or women.

   J Job titles change, but this doesn't mean that the job itself has changed.

3. What is a main difference between a summary and a paraphrase?

   A A summary is not in your own words, but a paraphrase is.

   B A paraphrase includes details, but a summary does not.

   C A paraphrase is a copy, but a summary is in your own words.

   D A summary includes details, but a paraphrase does not.

4. A summary can best be defined as

   F a restatement of a passage in your own words

   G the main idea of a passage plus several details

   H a restatement of text that includes details

   J the main idea of a passage, stated in your own words

5. A paraphrase can best be defined as

   A a restatement of a passage in your own words

   B the main idea of a passage plus one or two details

   C a restatement of a passage that does not include details

   D the main idea of a passage, stated in your own words

Using Supporting Evidence

When you express an opinion in writing, you must support it with evidence. **Supporting evidence** may be facts, statistics, examples, or reasons. Any details that do not directly support the opinion should be left out.

Read each opinion. Place a checkmark (√) next to each fact, statistic, example, or reason that supports it.

1. Rachel Carson's writings helped make people aware of environmental issues.

   ___ **A** She wrote conservation bulletins for the government.

   ___ **B** Her book *Silent Spring* was recommended by the president's science advisers.

   ___ **C** She earned a college degree in biology.

   ___ **D** *Silent Spring* is said to have begun the modern environment movement.

   ___ **E** A newspaper columnist said that *Silent Spring* encouraged the world to take a "new direction."

2. Many teenagers have money to spend and are valuable shoppers.

   ___ **F** A national poll showed that the average teenager's allowance is $50 per week.

   ___ **G** Teenagers usually do not have household expenses, so they have choices about how they spend.

   ___ **H** Companies spend billions of dollars every year advertising to teenagers.

   ___ **J** Studies show that teenagers spend most of their money on entertainment, clothing, and impulse purchases.

   ___ **K** Teenagers of today are exposed to more violence than those of earlier times.

Practice

Read each opinion. From the box, choose evidence that supports each opinion and write it on the lines below the opinion.

> Test animals go blind, lose fur, and develop tumors.
> Thousands of animals die each year, but only a few new drugs are produced.
> New drugs are needed to save people's lives.
> Researchers give test animals clean, safe places to live and plenty to eat.
> Test animals are imprisoned and do not live a natural life.
> Test animals would die sooner in the wild or as homeless strays.
> No one can prove that these animals actually suffer pain like people do.
> Animals have rights just as people do, but they cannot speak for themselves.

1. Testing new drugs on animals causes suffering and should be stopped.

_____

_____

_____

_____

_____

_____

2. We must test new drugs on animals in order to improve life for people.

_____

_____

_____

_____

_____

_____

Apply

For each opinion, add three pieces of supporting evidence. You can make up statistics.

1. High schools should not have dress codes.

   A

   _____

   _____

   B

   _____

   _____

   C

   _____

   _____

2. Nursing homes should keep several cats and dogs as pets.

   A

   _____

   _____

   B

   _____

   _____

   C

   _____

   _____

Check Up

Circle the answer for each question.

1. Students should be able to use calculators during their math tests.

   Which of the following supports this opinion?

   A It is important to check the answer that a calculator gives to make sure it is correct.

   B The point of taking math is to be able to think through problems.

   C Students will stop thinking and become too dependent on machines.

   D In real life, everyone uses calculators to make basic computations.

2. Wetlands in the United States should be preserved and protected from pollution.

   Which of the following supports this opinion?

   F Wetlands are swamps with many poisonous creatures.

   G Wetlands are ecosystems that protect other ecosystems and help prevent flooding.

   H Each organism has a different role, or job.

   J People sometimes change ecosystems to meet their own needs and wants.

3. The speed limit should be reduced to 55 miles per hour nationwide.

   Which of the following supports this opinion?

   A Studies show that the lowest number of fatal accidents occur where the speed limit is 55.

   B Mass transportation in the nation needs to be expanded.

   C Some people will always break the law and speed, no matter what the speed limit.

   D Since people always go 10 miles over the speed limit, 55 is reasonable.

4. There should be a government agency to prevent crime on the Internet.

   Which of the following supports this opinion?

   F Government agencies have not proven to be effective in the past.

   G The Internet has grown too large, too fast.

   H Thousands of people lose money to Internet crime every week.

   J Everyone should be guaranteed access to the Internet.

Read On As you read "African-American Soldiers: Unsung Heroes," look for evidence to support opinions that are expressed. Then answer the questions.

Review

Characters

Writers make **characters** seem real through their words, thoughts, and actions. Writers also use the thoughts, words, and actions of other characters to show what a character is like. **Dynamic characters** change and grow. **Flat characters** stay the same.

Main Idea

The **main idea** is the most important idea in a paragraph. All details in a paragraph support the main idea.

Compare/Contrast

Writers **compare** things when they show how they are alike. When writers show how things are different, they **contrast** them.

Drawing Conclusions

When you make a judgment based on what you have read combined with your experiences, you **draw a conclusion**.

Cause and Effect

Writers use **cause and effect** to explain how one event causes another. Why something happens is the cause. What happens is the effect.

Summarizing and Paraphrasing

When you **summarize**, you use your own words to tell the main idea of a paragraph. When you **paraphrase**, you restate a paragraph in your own words and you include details.

Supporting Evidence

You support conclusions with facts and opinions.

Assessment

Circle the response that answers each question or completes each statement.

A housefly may look harmless, but it isn't. It is one of the dirtiest creatures on Earth. Flies lay their eggs in garbage, waste, and rotting flesh. They eat spoiled food. Each fly carries thousands of bacteria that can cause disease. Flies spread these germs to people when they land on food. These germ-carrying insects also reproduce very quickly. There's little that can be done to keep flies away.

1. What is the main idea of this paragraph?

   A Every housefly carries germs.

   B The housefly, far from being harmless, is a carrier of disease.

   C Houseflies reproduce quickly.

   D There is no way to get rid of houseflies.

2. From this paragraph you can conclude that

   F you should be careful not to let houseflies sit on food

   G you should not let food spoil

   H houseflies are harmless

   J houseflies only spread germs when they bite you

People used to make fires by rubbing two sticks together. This made friction that created heat. The heat caused burnable materials next to the sticks to catch fire. Matches work in the same way, but faster. Match tips are coated with chemicals. These chemicals spark and burn easily. When a match is struck against a surface, the friction makes the chemical spark. The spark then reacts quickly with the chemical to make a flame. The flame can then burn down the stick of the match.

3. In both cases, the spark is caused by

   A a flame

   B chemicals

   C friction

   D sticks

4. Choose the best summary of this passage.

   F The tips of matches are coated with chemicals.

   G All fires are started with matches.

   H Matches work in the same way as rubbing two sticks because of the heat caused by friction.

   J Matches light quickly because they are coated with chemicals.

Among honeybees, the worker bees are the busiest. In the first days of their adult lives, worker bees clean hives. They build the hive and guard it against danger. They fly from plant to plant in search of food. All workers bees are females. The queen is the head of the hive. Her job is to lay eggs in the spring. The only function of male bees, or drones, is to mate with the queen. Drones are present in the hive only during the summer. In the fall, when food becomes scarce, the workers stop feeding the drones. The workers then drag the drones out of the hive to die.

5. How are the worker bees and queen bees alike?

   A They lay eggs.

   B They gather food.

   C They are female bees.

   D They are in the hive only during the summer.

6. Which fact does **not** support the idea that worker bees are the busiest bees in the hive?

   F Worker bees clean the hive.

   G All worker bees are females.

   H Worker bees gather food.

   J Worker bees build and guard the hive.

Clara Barton set up the American Red Cross. She began her work during the Civil War. She cared for wounded soldiers. After the war, Barton set up a group to search for missing soldiers. On a trip to Switzerland, she learned about an international group of volunteers. They helped the wounded without regard to their nationality. This group was the International Red Cross. Barton wanted Americans to do the same thing. As a result, she set up the American Red Cross. It began giving relief in disasters other than war.

7. What word best describes Clara Barton?

   A selfish

   B artistic

   C caring

   D disorganized

8. Which sentence supports the fact that Barton was called the "Angel of the Battlefield"?

   F She cared for soldiers.

   G On a trip to Switzerland, she learned about an international group.

   H She wanted people to take part in Red Cross activities.

   J She provided relief in disasters other than war.

Sandstone can be like sandpaper. It can be used to make surfaces smooth. Sandstone is a rock made of sand and natural cement. The sand is made up of minerals. Sandstone is often used to sharpen metal tools. It can also grind down wooden objects. The sand particles in the stone stick out like tiny teeth. They give the rock a rough surface. Whetstones made of sandstone sharpen tools and smooth surfaces. Sandstone is so rough it can scrape the skin off your leg if you walk into a piece by accident.

9. This passage is about

   A different uses for sandpaper

   B how to sharpen tools

   C why people don't use sandstone any more

   D the uses of sandstone

10. Choose the best paraphrase of this paragraph.

   F Sandstone is a rock with sharp edges. You can use it to sharpen tools or wooden objects.

   G Minerals make up the rock called sandstone. The rock is so rough that it feels like it has teeth. You should be careful walking by sandstone.

   H Sandstone is made of different minerals. The rock has a rough surface. It can be used to grind metal or wood. Whetstones made of sandstone are used to sharpen tools and smooth rough surfaces.

   J Whetstones are used to sharpen tools. Whetstones are made of sandstone and can also make surfaces smooth.

11. In what way are sandstone and sandpaper alike?

   A They are both used to make whetstones.

   B They can both be used to cement things together.

   C They are both rocks.

   D They can both be used to smooth surfaces.

Different Perspectives

A photo caption is a sentence or short paragraph that briefly describes a photograph. Photos that appear in newspapers and magazines often have photo captions. Captions focus on certain details in the picture depending on the author's purpose. Look at the picture and follow the directions to write a photo caption.

Write sentences, using the author's purpose and point of view stated for each of the following items.

1. Write a sentence that tells when and where the race was held. Also tell who won the race.
    Author's Purpose: to inform the reader about the race
    Author's Point of View: third person

    _____

    _____

    _____

2. Write a sentence that tells what the winner said after the race. Remember to use quotation marks.
    Author's Purpose: to tell the reader who won the race
    Author's Point of View: first person

    _____

    _____

    _____

3. Write a sentence that tells why people should run or do other exercise.
    Author's Purpose: to persuade the reader about the benefits of exercise
    Author's Point of View: third person

    _____

    _____

    _____

Exaggerated Language

Hyperbole is a literary device that uses exaggerated statements as a form of figurative language.

It was hot enough to fry an egg on the sidewalk.

Its purpose is to entertain, not misinform, the reader. Hyperbole is often funny; it can be found in comic strips, cartoons, on TV, and at the movies.

Use hyperbole to answer each of the questions.

1. How small is Center City?

   _____

   _____

2. How bad was the rush hour traffic this morning?

   _____

   _____

3. How mean is your friend's cat?

   _____

   _____

4. How crowded was the subway?

   _____

   _____

5. How bad is the condition of your uncle's car?

   _____

   _____

Predicting Outcomes

A writer gives clues that help you predict what might happen next. Deciding what you think will happen next is called **predicting outcomes.** As you read, think about what you know so far. What is likely to happen next?

A character will continue to act in a consistent way. For example, if a character named Tom is usually curious, you can predict what he will do when he sees an odd-shaped box sitting on the table: He will look inside.

For each passage, circle the answer that tells what is most likely to happen next.

1.   Five-year-old Allie is afraid of the dark. She is staying overnight at a friend's house for the first time. They are having fun with puppets. Suddenly, the power goes off.

   A Allie and her friend will use a flashlight to play shadow puppets.

   B Allie will be afraid and ask to go home.

   C Allie will tell her friend ghost stories.

2.   Tyler wants a motorcycle badly. He reads motorcycle magazines all the time. He saves his money and dreams of buying a motorcycle. Tyler is 17, and his parents have told him he cannot have a motorcycle until he is 18. Then one day he sees an ad in the paper. The motorcycle he wants is for sale. He has enough money saved to pay for it.

   F Tyler will decide he doesn't want the motorcycle after all.

   G Tyler's parents will buy the motorcycle for him.

   H Tyler will show his parents the ad and try to persuade them to let him buy it.

3.   Anita is very shy. While others chat and laugh at the bus stop, she just waits quietly. Anita has a crush on Hank. He is always surrounded by friends. Then one day she gets to the bus stop early. Hank and she are the only two people there.

   A Anita will start a lively conversation with Hank.

   B Anita will wait quietly and hope that Hank will speak to her.

   C Hank will ask Anita on a date that night.

Practice

Read each passage. Circle the answer that tells what is most likely to happen next.

1. Kipper is a Siamese cat. He loves playing with his owners. Every evening, when they get home at six o'clock, they get out a ball of yarn and a toy mouse. Kipper plays hard for 15 minutes and then wants dinner. Today, Kipper's owners are a little late coming home from work.

    A When they arrive, Kipper is missing.

    B When they arrive, Kipper is sleeping.

    C When they arrive, Kipper is ready to play.

2. Jeannine likes to keep busy. She enjoys being around people. All school year, she was active in after-school clubs. She especially liked the Science Club. Now that summer vacation has come, she is bored. Her mother shows her the Park District summer program brochure.

    F Jeannine will look for a science activity offered by the Park District.

    G Jeannine will complain that there is nothing to do.

    H Jeannine will sleep late and watch TV every day.

3. Emmanuel is an exchange student from Spain. He has spent a year living with the Wright family in the Midwest. Now the Wrights seem like his own family to him. Chris Wright is like a brother to him. Though Emmanuel is glad to be going home, he knows he will miss his American family.

    A Emmanuel will soon forget about the Wrights.

    B Emmanuel will stay in touch with the Wrights and write to Chris often.

    C The Wright family will send Emmanuel lots of gifts over the next year.

4. Kyle and Chad are teen-aged brothers. They are very different from each other. So they often disagree and argue. Deep down, however, they love each other. They feel loyalty to each other. One day, Kyle hears someone making fun of Chad behind his back.

    F Kyle can't wait to get home and mock Chad.

    G Kyle joins in and makes fun of Chad, too.

    H Kyle has angry words with the outsider who is making fun of his brother.

Apply

Read each passage. Choose the sentence that tells what probably happens next. On the blank line, write a sentence telling why you think this will happen.

1.   José has track practice after classes every day. The team is getting ready for a big meet. Practices have been long and hard. Today José is especially tired, hot, and thirsty after practice. He goes home right after practice.

   A José calls up his friends as soon as he gets home.

   B José drinks lots of water and takes a cool shower right away.

   C José has a big dinner as soon as he gets home.

   _____

2.   Katrina's parents own a drug store. Katrina likes spending time at the store. She admires the way her parents have made it a success. Katrina especially likes the gift section of the store. This summer, Katrina wants a job.

   F Katrina will ask her parents if she can work in the gift section of their store.

   G Katrina will fill out a job application for the grocery store next door.

   H Katrina will ask her parents where they think she could get a job.

   _____

3.   Alan likes high adventure and thrills. He has been backpacking in the mountains. He has been white-water rafting. He is always the first to try new roller coasters. Alan will graduate from high school this June. His parents have offered him a trip anywhere in the world as his graduation present.

   A Alan will ask for a trip to Hollywood so he can see movies being filmed.

   B Alan will ask for a trip to New York City so he can visit the Statue of Liberty.

   C Alan will ask for a trip to Brazil so he can canoe down the Amazon.

   _____

Check Up

Read the passages and circle the answer for each question.

1.   It is getting dark. Hannah is nervous. She is watching for her guests. They are runaway slaves. She is ready to feed six people and hide them in her house tonight. Hannah knows this is dangerous, but she is determined to do the right thing. She knows slavery is wrong.

What probably happens next?

A Hannah loses her nerve and locks the door.

B Hannah feeds the runaways but will not let them stay the night.

C Hannah changes her mind and turns the runaways over to the sheriff.

D Hannah overcomes her fear and welcomes the runaways into her home.

2.   Paul and Melika always have a date on Friday. Paul picks up Melika at 7:00 P.M., and they go to a 7:30 P.M. movie. This Friday, Paul has to work overtime and is running late. When he gets out of the shower, it is already 7:00 P.M.

What probably happens next?

F Paul calls Melika and tells her he will be a little late.

G Paul decides to call off the date and stays home.

H Melika is angry that Paul is late and cancels the date.

J Paul reads his e-mail and then leaves to pick up Melika.

3.   Today is Nicole's 21st birthday. She is surprised and hurt that no one has made a fuss over it. Her parents just called and said, "Happy Birthday. Your gift will be coming late." Her roommate Susan gave her a card but no gift. She won't even have a cake, she thinks in dismay. In fact, Susan had said that morning she wouldn't be home until late tonight. As Nicole unlocks the apartment door, she thinks she hears whispering.

What probably happens next?

A Nicole has a quiet dinner and goes to bed early.

B Nicole's friends and family jump out and yell "Surprise!"

C Nicole makes up her mind to celebrate by herself.

D Nicole's roommate brings her a cake when she comes home later.

4.   Raul is a person who takes pride in doing things right and on time. He likes everything to go according to plan. Raul is put in charge of the company picnic this year.

What probably happens next?

F Raul forgets to buy any food for the picnic.

G Raul asks someone else to plan the picnic.

H Raul gets right to work planning a perfect picnic.

J Raul can't think what to do next.

More Predicting Outcomes

Your life experience helps you understand stories. Use what you have read and what you already know to predict what will happen next in a story.

> Grandma has been poor all her life. She dreams of becoming rich suddenly. She buys a lottery ticket every day. She sends in the sweepstakes entry forms that come in the mail. A man calls today and tells her she has won $50,000 but she must send in $100 to hold her prize.

STORY CLUES: Grandma longs to win a lot of money. She is always buying lottery tickets and sending in sweepstakes entries.

EXPERIENCE CLUES: Very few people win anything from the lottery or sweepstakes. Millions of people believe what they want to believe, not what is likely.

PREDICTION: Grandma will send the man $100 and will lose her money because the offer is fake.

Read the following story. Use what you read and what you know to predict what might happen next.

> Adam is baby-sitting with eight-year-old Tara. Adam is very responsible and is an excellent baby-sitter. He and Tara are baking cookies. Adam carefully shows Tara what to do at each step. She wants to do everything by herself. The cookies go in the oven. Adam says, "I will take the hot trays out when it is time. They are too hot for a little girl to handle!" But Adam is on the phone when the timer goes off.

STORY CLUES:

_____

_____

EXPERIENCE CLUES:

_____

_____

PREDICTION:

_____

Practice

Use clues from each story and what you already know to predict what is likely to happen next. Circle the sentence that best predicts the outcome.

1. Walt daydreams often. He finds it hard to pay attention in class. As he listens to the history lesson about World War II, he daydreams about being an Air Force pilot. He draws pictures of planes on his paper. At the end of class, he has taken no notes.

    A Walt's illustrations are used for a bulletin board display on World War II planes.

    B Walt cannot answer the quiz questions the teacher asks the next day.

    C Walt receives an A on his slide presentation on World War II planes.

2. Barb loves animals, but she hasn't taken care of her pets. Her goldfish died because she didn't get around to changing their water. She had to give away her hamster because she forgot to feed it and clean its cage. She begs for a puppy and promises she will take care of it. Barb's parents get her a puppy for her birthday.

    F Barb's mom soon finds herself feeding and caring for the puppy.

    G Barb takes good care of the puppy, and they are always together.

    H Barb loses interest in animals soon after.

3. Brett is a class clown. He loves making people laugh and being the center of attention. Today the drama coach posted a sign. It announces tryouts for the spring play. The play is a musical comedy.

    A Brett attends the musical and enjoys it.

    B Brett tries out for the musical and gets a role.

    C Brett makes fun of the students who try out for the musical.

4. Ami is a senior. She is a good student who has a B+ average. Her ACT and SAT scores are high. Ami is also the star goalie of the high school's women's soccer team. She applies for a scholarship to her state university.

    F Ami is awarded a scholarship.

    G Ami fails a course.

    H Ami decides not to go to college.

Apply

Use clues from the passage and what you already know to predict what might happen next.

1.   Jonelle has grown up next door to a horse stable. The manager, Mr. Pierce, let her help him clean stalls and groom and feed horses for years. He has taught her a great deal about the care of horses. He has begun to show her how to train young horses. Jonelle is now 16 years old. Mr. Pierce has told her he has something special to ask her today.

What do you think Mr. Pierce will ask Jonelle?

_____

2.   Mr. Hupke's class has planned a picnic today. The food, games, and contests are ready. The sixth graders are excited. But this morning, the sky looks dark and angry with clouds. The forecast calls for thunderstorms.

What do you think Mr. Hupke and the sixth graders will do if it rains?

_____

3.   Beth and her older sister Anna like to borrow clothes from each other. Beth wants to wear Anna's red sweater tonight. But Anna has not come home yet, so Beth cannot ask her if it's all right to borrow the sweater. Anna has never said no to Beth, though.

What do you think Beth will do?

_____

4.   Matt is a hard-working young man. He is also a fast runner. Matt has trained hard for months for the race. Every week, he has run faster in the half-mile race. Today he will race against John, who has beaten Matt before but now has an injury.

Who do you think will win the race?

_____

Check Up

Read each passage and circle the answer for each question.

1. Martina buys a new dress to wear to the dance. She drops it on the way home and it gets dirty. She washes the dress without reading the care label. The label says "Dry Clean Only."

What do you think the outcome will be?

A Martina will look sharp in her new dress.

B The dirt will not come out of the dress.

C The new dress will shrink and be ruined.

D Martina's mom will be pleased that Martina solved her problem.

2. Carl and his friend Deniece have a dog-walking business. Today Carl is supposed to take the Jones family's three dogs out at 2:00 P.M. But his car breaks down, and he knows he will be very late. Carl knows the dogs must be taken for a walk. He uses his cell phone to make a call.

What do you think the outcome will be?

F The Jones family will fire him.

G Mr. Jones will leave work early to walk the dogs.

H Carl will call Deniece to ask if she will walk the dogs today.

J Carl will receive a bonus at the end of the week.

3. Hector invites a coworker to come to dinner. He decides he will cook a fancy meal and impress her. The day of the dinner, he chooses his recipes and buys the food. As he begins reading through the recipes, he discovers that he does not understand all the directions. He guesses. It is almost time for dinner, and Hector's dinner smells very odd.

What do you think the outcome will be?

A The dinner will be perfect and Hector's coworker will be impressed.

B Hector will produce some new foods and write a cookbook.

C Hector's dinner will not be very good.

D Hector will ask his coworker to help him cook something else.

Recognizing Fact and Opinion

A **fact** is a statement that can be proved true. For example, you could check a source such as an encyclopedia, atlas, or textbook to prove that it is true.

> **Fact:** The sun will set at 7:23 P.M. tonight.
> (Check in a newspaper.)

An **opinion** is a statement of belief or feelings. It cannot be proved.

> **Opinion:** This sunset is the most beautiful I have ever seen.

Write *O* beside each opinion. Write *F* beside each fact.

_____ 1. The Great Pyramid of Giza is 450 feet high.

_____ 2. The pyramid is one of the most inspiring sights on Earth.

_____ 3. Ancient Egypt had one of the greatest civilizations of all time.

_____ 4. Egyptians used papyrus, a form of paper made from a tall water reed.

_____ 5. Egyptian pyramids served as royal tombs.

_____ 6. Egyptian pharaohs were believed to be the sons of a god.

_____ 7. When a pharaoh died, he was buried with many treasures.

_____ 8. A mummy is spooky to look at.

_____ 9. Egyptian bodies were mummified, or preserved in salt and chemicals.

_____ 10. Our own way of preserving bodies is not as good as the ancient Egyptian method.

Practice

Write *F* beside each fact and *O* beside each opinion. If the statement is a fact, write the name of one resource in which you could find information to prove the fact. Choose among these sources: encyclopedia, atlas, dictionary, or daily newspaper.

_____   **1.** Texas is the largest state in the United States.

_____

_____   **2.** The coastline of Maine is rocky.

_____

_____   **3.** Ben Franklin wanted the wild turkey to be our national bird.

_____

_____   **4.** The eagle is a cruel bird.

_____

_____   **5.** The colonial period was the most exciting era in U.S. history.

_____

_____   **6.** The Revolutionary War was fought between 1775 and 1783.

_____

_____   **7.** The Bay High Bengals won yesterday's football game.

_____

_____   **8.** Thomas Jefferson was the most brilliant of the colonial leaders.

_____

Apply

Read each passage. Cross out each opinion.

1.   The newspaper has been a part of American life for hundreds of years. Today everyone should read a daily paper from first page to last page. The *Los Angeles Times* and the *New York Times* are two major newspapers that are highly respected.

2.   The first page of a newspaper has the headlines. These announce the day's most important stories. The editorial section contains comments and opinions written by editors and readers. Some letters to the editor are ridiculous.

3.   The classified ads tell about jobs and things for sale. These ads provide a service for newspaper readers. You should always check the classified ads so you don't miss the bargains!

4.   The funnies are the best part of the whole paper. A number of cartoon strips appear in the newspaper every day. Cartoons that are very popular appear in hundreds of papers around the country.

5.   To find your way around a newspaper, look for a table of contents. It is often on the bottom of the first or second page. Page numbers for regular features are shown here. Our paper recently changed the style of its table of contents. The new style is much nicer than the old one.

Check Up

Circle the answer for each question.

1. Which of the following is a fact?

   A Wild cats are the most beautiful animals in the world.

   B A cheetah is the world's fastest animal.

   C A jaguar is sneaky.

   D The lion is truly the king of the beasts.

2. Which of the following is an opinion?

   F Many people still go to see movies at a theater.

   G Some movie theater business has been lost to videos.

   H There is nothing like seeing a first-run film on the big screen.

   J Hollywood still produces most U.S. films.

3. Which of the following is a fact?

   A Puerto Rico should become the fifty-first state.

   B Puerto Rico is a wonderful vacation destination.

   C Puerto Rico offers everything the traveler could want.

   D Puerto Rico is an island.

4. Which of the following is an opinion?

   F California has a large population compared to Utah.

   G Thousands of people have moved to California in the past ten years.

   H California is a more important state than New York.

   J Many computer companies are located in California.

5. Which of the following is a fact?

   A The plots of *West Side Story* and *Romeo and Juliet* are similar.

   B Both stories make everyone cry.

   C Leonard Bernstein, who composed the music for *West Side Story*, was a genius.

   D Natalie Wood was perfect as Maria in the movie.

6. Which of the following is an opinion?

   F There are six time zones in the United States.

   G From east to west, the zones are Eastern, Central, Mountain, Pacific, Alaska, and Hawaii-Aleutian.

   H Railroad company executives created the idea of standard time in 1883.

   J We couldn't exist without standard time in our busy society.

Identifying Fact and Opinion

Many people have strong opinions. To persuade others to agree with them, they offer facts to support their opinions. Here is an example.

OPINION:
People who live in apartments should not own dogs.

SUPPORTING FACTS:
Dogs need exercise and fresh air daily.
Dogs in apartments spend most of their time inside.
Dog waste on city streets and sidewalks is a problem.

Decide which facts support each opinion. Write them on the lines below the opinion.

FACTS: Many athletes demand salaries in the millions.
Many athletes do a lot of charity work.
Many athletes work daily to keep their bodies in shape.
Some athletes use illegal drugs.
Some athletes get into trouble with the law.
Many people are inspired by athletes.

OPINION 1: Today's pro athletes are good role models.

_____

_____

_____

OPINION 2: Today's pro athletes are poor role models.

_____

_____

_____

Practice

Read each opinion. Below each opinion are four statements. Some are facts and some are opinions. Circle the fact that best supports the opinion.

1. Workers should not be forced to retire at age 65.

   A It is a crime to force workers into early retirement.

   B Retirement is boring.

   C It isn't fair to force people to live on less money.

   D Many workers over 65 can do the same job as younger workers.

2. Our city should sponsor a late night basketball program.

   F Curfew for teenagers 17 and under is 11:00 P.M. on weeknights.

   G Gang activity has decreased in two communities that have already created such programs.

   H Basketball is fun.

   J It is cool to play basketball late at night.

3. Bicyclists and motorcyclists should wear helmets.

   A Helmets look cool.

   B Wearing helmets has been shown to reduce serious injuries in accidents by 60 percent.

   C I don't know anyone who has been hurt riding a bike without a helmet.

   D Each person should have the right to make up his or her own mind about wearing a helmet.

4. The six-acre woods next to the city park should be bought by the park district.

   F Everybody likes to walk in the park.

   G The woods is prime real estate and might easily cost millions of dollars.

   H Buying the woods would enlarge public natural space and preserve wildlife habitats.

   J The park district's budget should be increased to pay forest preserve expenses.

5. The speed limit on highways should be 55 miles per hour.

   A Today's cars are designed so they can travel fast.

   B Studies show that 50 percent fewer accidents occur when the speed limit is 55 than when it is 70 miles per hour.

   C Modern cars can travel many miles on one gallon of gas.

   D Trucks have to go 50 miles per hour.

Apply

For each opinion, choose a fact from the box that supports the opinion.

> Eleanor Roosevelt chaired the Human Rights Commission in the 1940s.
> About 13 million Americans travel to Canada for fun every year.
> Eleanor Roosevelt wrote a daily newspaper column.
> In 1997, almost 70 percent of 18 to 24 year olds had computer hobbies.
> Canada has much wilderness and wildlife.
> Tom Hanks was born in California.
> About 38 percent of 18 to 24 year olds do volunteer work.
> Mosquitoes spread diseases such as malaria and encephalitis.
> Tom Hanks won the academy Award for Best Actor two years in a row.
> Only female mosquitoes bite.

1. Young adults are interested in helping others.

    _____

2. Tom Hanks is a great actor.

    _____

3. Eleanor Roosevelt was concerned about people and their rights.

    _____

4. Canada is a popular vacation spot for travelers from the United States.

    _____

5. The mosquito is a harmful insect.

    _____

Check Up

Read each opinion. Then circle the statement that best supports the opinion.

1. Stronger pollution control laws for cars are needed to protect the air.

   A The Clean Air Acts required auto makers to reduce pollution emitted by cars.

   B In the 1960s, Ralph Nader published *Unsafe at Any Speed*.

   C Cars and other means of transportation produce almost 80 percent of the carbon monoxide in the air.

   D Chlorofluorocarbons can break down the ozone layer.

2. Dogs and people have lived together for a long time.

   F Some dogs are trained to help people with disabilities.

   G Dogs have good senses of smell and hearing.

   H Like human babies, puppies are helpless at birth.

   J Fossils of humans and dogs that are about 10,000 years old have been found together.

3. Adults complain about children watching too much TV, but they watch more television than kids do.

   A In the late 1990s television networks set up a ratings system for programs.

   B Political candidates advertise on television.

   C Children average less than 24 hours of watching TV a week; adults average from 20 to over 40 hours a week.

   D *ER* was the top-rated regularly scheduled network television program during the 1998–1999 season.

4. It appears that many people today are coming to the United States from Latin America.

   F Minnesota has more people of Norwegian ancestry than any other state.

   G In 1990 most immigrants from Ecuador lived in the Northeast.

   H In 1990 almost 43 percent of immigrants came from Latin America.

   J In 1850 almost 21,000 immigrants came from Latin America.

Read On   Read "A Walk Through the Rain Forest." Answer the questions and look for facts and opinions.

Recognizing Author's Purpose

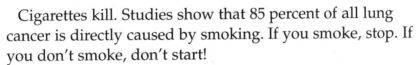

Each author has a purpose, or reason, for writing. The most common purposes are the following:

- to describe something
- to give information or explain
- to persuade
- to tell a story

> Cigarettes kill. Studies show that 85 percent of all lung cancer is directly caused by smoking. If you smoke, stop. If you don't smoke, don't start!

The purpose of this writing is to persuade you to avoid smoking.

Read each passage. Write *persuade, inform or explain, describe,* or *tell a story* to tell the author's purpose.

1. The Badlands of South Dakota look like another planet. The rock is carved into fantastic ridges, cliffs, and canyons. The ridges stretch as far as the eye can see. In the hot sun, everything ripples with heat. There are no trees or grass.

   The author's purpose is to _____.

2. A green plant is a factory for making its own food. The plant uses energy from sunlight. This energy acts on materials to change them. Water molecules are split. Hydrogen and carbon dioxide molecules are joined to produce a sugar.

   The author's purpose is to _____.

3. Lisa knew this race would be different. She had been training hard day after day. Her coach had said yesterday, "Lisa, this race will be yours to win." Now she was standing at the starting line next to Debra. She had never beaten Debra.

   The author's purpose is to _____.

4. If you haven't joined the Harry Potter fan club, it's time you did. These books about the young wizard are fascinating and well-written, too. They combine magic, suspense, and mystery. But best of all, they grab you with their skillful story-telling. So settle down with one of the Harry Potter books tonight.

   The author's purpose is to _____.

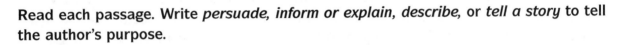

Practice

Read each passage. Write *persuade, inform or explain, describe,* or *tell a story* to tell the author's purpose.

1. Our community needs a girls' soccer club. Over the past ten years, the school soccer program for girls has grown 250 percent. But it operates only in the spring. To compete, we need to offer training and practice for girls year-round.

    The author's purpose is to _____.

2. To start the mower, first turn the throttle to Choke. Press down on the gas pedal three times. Then turn on the ignition. As the engine warms, turn the throttle counterclockwise to decrease the gas flow. The engine should run smoothly.

    The author's purpose is to _____.

3. Our vacation was doomed from the start. As we headed out the driveway, we had a flat tire. The first night, we couldn't find a motel room. It seems there was a fishing derby going on in the region. All the motel rooms for miles were full. We finally found a run-down place after midnight. By then, it had started to rain.

    The author's purpose is to _____.

4. The rough-coated collie has a flat skull and a long snout. Its small ears stand up. Its tail is rather long and is usually carried low.

    The author's purpose is to _____.

5. Sometimes strange objects fall from the sky. These events are called skyfalls. Skyfalls may rain coins, fish, or frogs. Scientists can't explain how this happens. Some think that strong winds pick things up in one place and then drop them in another.

    The author's purpose is to _____.

Apply

Sometimes an author may have more than one purpose. The main purpose might be to inform, but the author may use description to help.

Read each passage. Write an *A* beside the author's main purpose. Write a *B* beside the author's secondary purpose.

1.   It takes only ten days for some flies to grow up. After one day in their eggs, these young flies hatch into wormlike larvae. These colorless creatures, also called grubs, can be found in rotting matter. The grubs eat, shed their skins, keep eating, and grow new skins. Then they enter the ground and become pupae. In the pupa state, they grow the legs and wings of adult flies.

The author's purposes are to

describe   _____

inform   _____

2.   I squirmed as I sat in the dentist's chair. With every poke and prod and scrape, I wished I had brushed and flossed more often. "A little more plaque than there ought to be here," said Dr. Gunnar. "Uhhhhhh," I groaned. Brush three times a day, floss once a day, don't eat between meals. As I left, I chanted this mantra to myself. I swear next time my teeth will be sparkling.

The author's purposes are to

tell a story   _____

persuade   _____

3.   It has a head like a horse, a tail like a monkey, and a pouch like a kangaroo. What strange creature is this? Why, it's the seahorse. A seahorse is not really a horse, of course. It is a peculiar little fish that travels in an upright position. Seahorses spend a lot of time clinging to seaweed, with their flexible tails wrapped around a piece of eelgrass or rockweed.

The author's purposes are to

describe   _____

inform   _____

Check Up

Read each passage and circle the answer for each question.

1.   Why is a book of maps called an atlas? Atlas was the name of a Greek god who held the heavens up on his shoulders. Artists showed him carrying a globe or holding the earth on his shoulders. A Flemish mapmaker put a picture of Atlas holding the globe on the cover of the book of maps he published in 1636. The practice became popular. Since then, books of maps have been called atlases.

The author's main purpose in this passage is to

A   persuade

B   inform or explain

C   tell a story

D   describe

2.   Beside the word *ugly* in the dictionary, there should be a picture of a toad. It surely is one of the ugliest creatures on the earth. Its rough skin is covered with warts, knobs, and creases. Its middle is fat. Its legs are squatty. Its eyes never blink, and they stick up like lamps above the long, grim slash of its mouth.

The author's main purpose in this passage is to

F   persuade

G   inform or explain

H   tell a story

J   describe

3.   We must put up a stoplight at the corner of Linden Street and Rolfe Road. Drivers proceeding along Linden often fail to obey the stop sign. They think that oncoming traffic is going to turn. Most cars do, but that is a foolish and deadly bet. Yesterday, yet another accident happened there. How many people have to get hurt before the city council does the right thing?

The author's main purpose in this passage is to

A   persuade

B   inform or explain

C   tell a story

D   describe

Recognizing Author's Effect and Intention

Once an author decides on one or more **purposes** (for example, to entertain, inform, persuade, or express feelings), he or she decides what attitude to take to the audience. For example, an **author's intention** may be to tell readers how to build a bookcase. For that goal, a straightforward, no-nonsense approach is probably most effective.

Style techniques like word choices, images, and figurative language help writers communicate their **tone**, or attitude toward their subject. These elements help readers identify the **author's effect**. An author's tone may be helpful, angry, funny, sarcastic, objective, or any of a dozen others.

> Lynn went to a speed-dating session. She knew the minute she walked into the restaurant that she should have just spent the evening talking to her cat. The first guy she met couldn't talk about anything but his mother. The second was still mad at his ex-wife. The third stared at her without blinking for the entire conversation. How can five minutes take longer than watching paint dry, she wondered.

In this passage, the writer uses phrases like *talking to her cat* and *watching paint dry* to create a sense of amusement. So the effect of the passage is to make readers laugh, and the author's tone could be described as funny, or humorous.

Read the passage. Circle the answer to each question.

> The most frightening moment of my life occurred while I was driving up the Dan Ryan Expressway in Chicago. Traffic was going 80 miles an hour, cars were merging into my lane from both directions, and suddenly my car hit a bump and the keys fell out of the ignition. I groped around on the floor for the key, expecting the car to die, all the while driving 75 to keep from being rear-ended. My heart was pounding so loud I couldn't hear the radio.

1. What is the author's tone in the passage?

   A angry

   B suspenseful

   C informational

   D sarcastic

2. Which words best communicate the author's tone?

   F life, die, heart

   G merging, bump, rear-ended

   H traffic, driving, ignition

   J frightening, die, pounding

Practice

Read each passage. Circle the word that best expresses the author's effect. It may help to underline any words and images in the passage that express the tone.

1.   To make broccoli pasta salad, first boil the pasta according to package directions. You can use egg noodles or rotini or anything you prefer. Then wash and trim the broccoli and cut it into pieces less than two inches square.

    A humorous

    B suspenseful

    C informational

    D sarcastic

2.   Tom jingled the coins in his pocket. Then he looked at his watch again. Where was that taxi? If he didn't get to the interview on time, he'd never get the job.

    F happy

    G impatient

    H sad

    J relaxed

Read each passage. Write a word that describes the effect the author is aiming for in the passage.

3.   Shelley was sitting on the carpeted floor in the lotus position. She closed her eyes for a moment and took a deep breath. Then she gazed into the candle flame in front of her. As the scent of lavender filled her senses, her cares floated away.

_____

4.   Speedometers have been around even longer than cars. They're based on the odometer, which dates back 2,000 years. The ancient Roman armies rolled a wheel as they marched and counted how many times it revolved. By the sixteenth century, the odometer had been combined with a clock.

_____

5.   Carrie looked in the mirror for the tenth time. She hardly recognized the girl who looked back. She didn't usually wear makeup or style her hair. But tonight was her first date ever. Jeffrey, who sat next to her in English class, had asked her to the movies, just the two of them. The doorbell rang. She waved jauntily at herself, then twirled, and ran down the stairs.

_____

Apply

Use the information in the flyer to answer the questions that follow.

Power Tool Safety Class

Do you work with power tools?
Don't wind up in the ER.

Steady Steel, the premier manufacturer of power tools, is offering a class on power tool safety. Our instructors are the best in the business. They've seen every possible danger, and they know how to avoid them. If you use any power tools, from chainsaw to table saw, for work or hobby, this class is for you. A small investment of $40 (just $10 per session) could save you thousands in medical bills.

Classes will run for four weeks starting March 21, every Wednesday night from 7:00 to 8:30 P.M., at the Donegal Community Center. Call (724) 555-9876 for directions or to ask questions.

Register Today!
Class size is limited to 15 students.
Call (724) 555-9876 to register.

---

1. The flyer says that class size is limited to 15 students in order to

   A suggest that not many people need this class

   B discourage people from registering

   C encourage people to register early

   D reassure shy people they won't be scared

2. The flyer says the instructors are "the best in the business" to

   F attract more participants

   G intimidate possible participants

   H justify the high prices of its tools

   J suggest that power-tool safety is a booming business

3. The flyer mentions medical bills to

   A complain about the high cost of health care

   B remind readers to pay their insurance premiums

   C argue that you should need a license to use power tools

   D emphasize that the class is a good investment

4. To what audience might Steady Steel send this flyer?

   F road crews

   G computer technicians

   H construction workers

   J scientists

Check Up

Read the passage. Then circle the answer to each question.

1   Maria was taking a peaceful walk in the woods on a bright October day. Since she had moved from Mexico City to the countryside in Ohio, she had had to work to learn a lot of things and get used to new surroundings. But she had felt right at home in the woods.

2   Suddenly she heard frantic barking. Before she could move, a huge brown dog came running up to her, growling. He jumped up and down in front of her, looking fierce.

3   Maria thought for a minute. She didn't have a dog of her own, but she had become friendly with the neighbors' dog. Granted, Ruby was only about the size of the brown dog's head, but Maria had calmed her down several times.

4   "Here, Brutus," she called softly, making up a name that suited such a giant. She slowly reached out her hand and snapped her fingers. "Good boy!" Where's a raw steak when you need one, she thought.

5   Brutus was looking so confused that Maria laughed. That made him duck his head and whimper. She touched his head. He rubbed it against her hand. Then he leaned his whole body against her.

6   "You're just a big softie," Maria teased. "May I take a look at your collar?" He stood still while she read the tag.

1. The tone of paragraph 2 is
   - **A** humorous
   - **B** frightening
   - **C** informative
   - **D** bitter

2. The tone of paragraph 5 is
   - **F** touching
   - **G** sarcastic
   - **H** intimidating
   - **J** ashamed

3. Which words best communicate the author's overall tone?
   - **A** frantic, fierce
   - **B** work, learn
   - **C** Brutus, giant
   - **D** peaceful, calmed

4. The author's intention in the passage is
   - **F** to warn readers about the dangers of dogs
   - **G** to relate a touching experience
   - **H** to show the difficulties immigrants face
   - **J** to picture the serenity of woods

Making Generalizations

A **generalization** is a conclusion that applies to many people, events, or situations. Several facts or specific examples lead you to make a logical generalization. Generalizations can sum up what has been said or introduce what will be said. An example of a generalization is *All dogs are friendly*.

Look for these words that signal generalizations: *most, many, few, all, usually, generally, and typically*. Some generalizations do not use signal words.

Evidence: I watched all afternoon as owners took their dogs into a business called Dog Daze. I noticed that each dog came out with its fur trimmed and washed.

Generalization: All the dogs who visit Dog Daze come out trimmed and washed.

Read each passage and decide what generalization it allows you to make.

1. Highway accidents in which driver and passengers were not wearing seat belts led to deaths 65 percent of the time last year in our county. Among those who were wearing seat belts, deaths occurred just 30 percent of the time. National statistics show that the likelihood of death doubles for each 10 miles over 30 miles per hour when passengers do not wear seat belts.

    From this passage we can generalize that

    A many lives would be saved if people wore seat belts

    B few people wear seat belts

    C highway accidents are caused by speeding

2. Some people in eastern Asia make a paste out of mashed termites. This is normally served with meals. Other people eat roasted locusts and grasshoppers. In Mexico, people eat ant candy. First they feed the ants honey. Then they remove the heads and legs and eat the honey-filled bodies. For a special treat, they dip the ants in chocolate first.

    From this passage we can generalize that

    F many people around the world eat bugs

    G locusts and grasshoppers are the most popular bugs

    H only poor people eat bugs

Practice

Read each paragraph and choose a generalization you can make using evidence in the paragraph.

1. An elephant uses its trunk to smell the air. It also uses its trunk to carry food and water to its mouth. It can even give itself a shower by shooting a stream of water from its trunk. The elephant can lift heavy loads by wrapping its trunk around them. The sensitive tip of an elephant's trunk allows the animal to feel the shapes and textures of objects. Finally, the elephant uses its trunk to caress its mate and young.

   From this passage we can generalize that the elephant's trunk

   A is amazingly strong and useful

   B grows rapidly after the elephant is born

   C is easily injured

2. Elephants stay close to each other in herds. They defend each other if the herd is attacked. The strong elephants make a circle around the young and weak ones to protect them. They also protect each other when they become sick and old. And if one elephant is injured, another will try to carry it to safety.

   From this passage we can generalize that elephants

   F usually attack other animals for no reason

   G are always loyal to fellow herd members

   H spend all of their time defending the herd

3. Fish live in rivers, lakes, streams, and the ocean. They have streamlined bodies and fins that help them move through the water. They have gills for taking in oxygen from water.

   From this passage we can generalize that fish

   A move very quickly

   B are easy to tame

   C always live in water

4. Owls cough up pellets after eating. The pellets often contain feathers, hair, beaks, and bones. Owl experts examine these pellets to learn about the owl. They pull them apart to see just what the owl has been eating.

   From this passage we can generalize that owls

   F eat things they should not eat

   G usually can't digest every part of the animals they eat

   H rarely eat other birds

Apply

Read each passage. Then complete the sentence telling what generalization it allows you to make.

1.   Harry plays on the high school soccer team in fall. In winter and spring, he plays on a team club. He attends at least two soccer camps in summer. Harry subscribes to three soccer magazines. The walls of his room are covered with posters of his favorite pro soccer players.

From this passage, I can generalize that Harry always

_____

2.   The Smith's dog Tuffy eats premium dog food every day. Tuffy has a healthy, shiny coat and bright eyes. He enjoys playing and going for walks with the Smiths every afternoon for an hour. He has lots of energy and is friendly and relaxed with people.

From this passage, I can generalize that Tuffy's owners usually

_____

3.   The radio station WZIG plays oldies from the 1960s, 70s, and 80s. WZIG advertises investment companies and retirement communities. The station holds contests about political trivia. Prizes are often trips or cruises. Most of the DJs are men and women in their 50s.

From this passage, I can generalize that most of the WZIG listeners

_____

4.   Tameeka reads three or four books a month. She belongs to a book club at the public library. Members meet every three weeks to discuss a novel they have read. Tameeka takes a book along with her on the train so that she can read on the way to and from work. She also reads during her lunch break.

From this passage, I can generalize that when Tameeka has free time, she usually

_____

Check Up

Circle the answer for each question.

1. Brent has completed his homework on time every week this year. He has earned As on quizzes and tests. Brent has made the straight-A honor roll every semester for the past three years.

   From this passage you can generalize that Brent

   A will succeed in life

   B overall is an excellent student

   C does not play any sports

   D has a photographic memory

2. Marna has three cats, two dogs, and a parakeet at home. She volunteers at the animal shelter one day a week. There she helps care for animals that have been abandoned. Marna also supports that local wildlife refuge shelter, which cares for injured and orphaned wild animals.

   From this passage you can generalize that Marna

   F has a job working with animals

   G never has time to spend with human friends

   H is always ready to care for animals in need

   J had no pets when she was growing up

3. Tucker will not walk under a ladder. If he steps on a crack in the sidewalk, he throws salt over his shoulder. He avoids black cats. Tucker has no mirrors on the walls of his house because he is afraid he might break one. That would mean seven years' bad luck.

   From this passage you can generalize that Tucker

   A is superstitious

   B is logical

   C has a great sense of humor

   D has no ladders in his home

4. Two musical groups held concerts at the Muldoon Center in Springfield last month. The city's pro basketball and hockey teams play their home games at the Muldoon Center. Conventions can book the center for large group meetings.

   From this passage you can generalize that when people need a big meeting center in Springfield

   F they frequently use the Muldoon Center

   G they build a new one

   H the Muldoon Center is always too busy for them

   J the Muldoon Center is too expensive for most of them

Read On   Read "How To Survive Anything." Look for generalizations about dangerous situations in the article. Then answer the questions.

Identifying Style Techniques

A writer's style is his or her own way of saying things. Ideally, style should fit the ideas being communicated. The words that are used, the types of sentences, and the organization should all work together.

Read this paragraph. Look for ways the writer has helped you feel Zach's fear.

> With each step up the ladder, Zach felt the cold pit in his stomach growing. His hands were tingling. The hair on the back of his neck prickled. The water looked a cold, steely blue. As it grew more distant, he wondered how he could force himself to continue. At last he reached the diving board.

The writer of this paragraph has chosen descriptive details to communicate Zach's fear of diving off the board. The short, choppy sentences add to the feeling of fear.

Read the following passage. Circle the answer that best identifies its style.

> A city dog went to the country to visit a country dog. He soon decided that all the farm dogs were cowards. They were afraid of a little black animal with a white stripe down its back. "You're all wimps!" the city dog exclaimed. "I can beat you and your friends. And I can beat the striped animal too. Lead me to him!"
>
> The farm dog said quietly, "Don't you want to ask any questions about it?"

1. "You're all wimps! I can beat you and your friends." By having the city dog speak using informal, slang words, the author

   A creates a serious mood

   B creates a casual mood

   C creates a mysterious mood

2. The writer has the animals speak. This technique

   F makes the animals seem like humans

   G makes the animals seem ridiculous

   H confuses most people who read the story

Practice

Read each passage. Then identify the style techniques that the author has used to extend meaning.

Julia's gown fitted her perfectly. She seemed to float down the stairs in a cloud of airy pink mist. Her glistening hair was swept up elegantly and held by a delicate silver clasp. Her skin glowed with health and the excitement of her first formal dance.

1. "She seemed to float down the stairs." In this sentence, the author means that Julia is

   A a little depressed

   B sad and scary

   C happy and excited

2. Phrases like *airy pink mist, swept up elegantly,* and *delicate silver clasp* help create a feeling of

   F stiff formality

   G fairy tale romance

   H scientific detail

3. By saying "her skin glowed," the author means Julia

   A was not wearing makeup

   B has been crying with happiness

   C has high color and is beaming

The cat's tongue is a tool with many uses. First, the sensitive feline tongue is used to taste food. Second, it acts as a spoon for scooping up liquids. Lapping with the curled tongue lets the cat drink its fill. Third, the cat's tongue acts as a washcloth. A cat can clean nearly every inch of its body using its tongue.

4. By saying the cat's tongue "acts as a spoon," the author means

   F it is hard and curved

   G it can form a bowl shape to hold liquid

   H the cat would find it easier to use a spoon

5. The author compares the cat's tongue to a washcloth because

   A both are used to clean the body

   B they look so much alike

   C the comparison is shocking

Apply

Read each passage. Circle the sentence that explains how the author used style techniques.

You're walking in the country on a crisp day in the late fall. In the distance you hear an unusual honking sound. It slowly grows nearer. You look up to see what is making the sound. There in the sky is a flock of long-winged, long-necked birds flying in a V-formation. They are geese, heading south for the winter.

1. The author has used descriptive details to

    A place you in a scene where geese appear

    B describe geese in detail

    C give interesting facts about geese

2. The phrase that helps you to see the geese best is

    F "an unusual honking sound"

    G "long-winged, long-necked birds flying in a V-formation"

    H "heading south for the winter"

The shrew is the animal kingdom's workaholic. He just can't seem to settle down and rest. No other animal rushes about in such a nonstop frenzy of industry. It dashes ahead with jerky movements, poking its sharp nose under every leaf. Why is the shrew the animal world's perpetual motion machine? To get food! The shrew's frantic activity uses up so much energy that it needs to eat almost constantly. To go without food for just a few hours means death.

3. The author calls the shrew "the animal kingdom's workaholic." By this, the author means

    A the shrew works without stopping except for sleep

    B the shrew is the only animal that works

    C the shrew eats almost all the time

4. Phrases like *frenzy of industry, jerky movements,* and *poking its sharp nose* create a feeling of

    F humor

    G peace

    H nervousness

Check Up

Read the passage. Then circle the answer for each question.

Imagine a sea animal that looks a lot like a pincushion with a great many pins sticking straight out. This is the sea urchin—a small, round creature covered with spines. The sea urchin is the porcupine of the sea. The spines are used both for protection and for locomotion. A sea urchin travels by stilting along on its waving spines. Though sea urchins appear harmless, they are best avoided. The ends of their spines are barbed, like fishhooks. This makes them very difficult to remove once they are embedded in the skin. The spines are very brittle, so they break off easily from the urchin. Some sea urchins also have a poison in their spines, which causes a painful sting like that of a hornet.

1. By comparing the sea urchin to a pincushion full of pins, the author means to describe

   A what the animal looks like

   B how the animal moves

   C the animal's bad temper

   D the animal's digestive system

2. By calling the sea urchin "the porcupine of the sea," the author makes it clear that

   F the urchin is well suited to life on land

   G the urchin is pretty and harmless

   H the urchin can use its spines as weapons

   J the urchin is good to eat

3. "A sea urchin travels by stilting along on its waving spines." This sentence shows that the urchin moves

   A as though on stilts

   B at a fast pace

   C by rolling from place to place

   D as little as possible

4. The author compares the ends of the spines to fishhooks. This picture helps you understand how the spines

   F are attached to the urchin

   G become fixed in an enemy or victim

   H make the urchin like a fish

   J can be freed from the urchin

5. To describe the sea urchin, the author mentions pincushions, porcupines, fishhooks, and hornets. The overall impression is that meeting a sea urchin would be

   A amusing

   B inspiring

   C terrifying

   D painful

Applying Passage Elements

Writers often use elements that allow you to learn more than just what their words have said. From these details you can "put two and two together" and extend the meaning of what you read. For example, read this passage:

> They call it the devilfish. This sea creature has wide fins that look like great wings and points that look like horns on its head. It also has a long, whiplike tail. One species of manta ray, called the Atlantic manta, grows to more than 23 feet. Superstitious fishermen fear them and think that a ray will wrap people in its huge wings and eat them.

A manta ray's body shape is probably
- **A** tall and thin
- **B** perfectly round
- **C** wide and flat

Describing the wide fins as huge wings helps you see that the fins extend for many feet on each side. Therefore, the ray's body must be **(C)** wide and flat.

Read the passage and use passage elements to extend meaning.

> The tailorbird of India lives up to its name when it makes its nest. First, the bird chooses two leaves that are growing near each other on a tree. Then, with its beak, it punches holes around the edges of the leaves. Using spider silk or long blades of grass, a male and a female tailorbird work together. The female stays between the leaves, while the male stays on the outside. The male pokes a piece of grass through one of the holes on a leaf. The female grabs it and pokes it back through a hole in the other leaf. This process continues until the two leaves have been sewn into a cup-shaped nest.

1. What does a tailor do?

   A conducts experiments

   B makes clothing

   C constructs buildings

2. The male and female tailorbird sew their nest. Their beaks are like

   F needles

   G thread

   H scissors

Practice

Read each passage. Underline the phrase that best completes each sentence.

It's tough to belong to a family of singers and not be able to carry a tune. Human beings aren't the only ones who have this problem. Sparrows are known as wonderful singers. The song sparrow sings some of the most beautiful bird songs in the world. But its cousin, the English sparrow, must have been born with a tin ear. It can barely even chirp on key.

1. *Born with a tin ear* is an expression that means someone

   A can't carry a tune

   B has to be careful of magnets

   C has ears made of metal

2. An English sparrow would not be valued by a bird watcher for its

   F wings

   G colors

   H song

A *pitcher's duel* is a baseball term. When a pitcher is throwing well, it is hard for the other team to get a hit. With no hits, there is no scoring. If both pitchers make it hard to get a hit, the game is called a pitcher's duel because they are controlling the game.

3. In a pitcher's duel, there will be a low

   A attendance

   B score

   C team spirit

When you hear the words *mold* and *fungus*, do you think of spoiled food? That thought is actually far from the whole truth. Mold is used in the making of many cheeses. For example, blue cheese is made with a blue mold. The mold gives the cheese its tangy flavor. Penicillin is also a mold. This mold cures infections and has saved many lives. Mushrooms are fungi that are edible and tasty.

4. Some molds and fungi are

   F dangerous to humans

   G harmless to humans

   H good for humans

Apply

Read each passage. Use what you have read and your common sense to extend the meaning. Then choose the sentence that tells what you can determine.

1. Fleas are only one-tenth of an inch long, but they can cause the animals they infest a lot of misery. When the flea needs food, it bites through the skin of the host animal and drains some blood. Between bites, it crawls around in the fur or jumps to another animal. The flea is an incredible jumper. If it were human size, the flea would be able to leap from the street to the tops of buildings.

    A A flea has a mighty impact for such a tiny creature.

    B Fleas are related to mosquitoes.

    C The flea and its host both benefit by the relationship.

2. A cowboy was a hired hand who rounded up beef cattle and drove them to market. His work took him over thousands of miles of grasslands and mountains every year. He spent long days in the saddle and often cooked and slept outdoors. With no shelter and only a fire for warmth, the cowboy often endured temperatures as low as 50 degrees below zero. In summer he worked a full day in the sun, no matter what the temperature.

    F A cowboy's job was much sought after by many young men.

    G The cowboy had to be tough and strong just to survive.

    H Men who loved to be outdoors in summer became cowboys.

3. Backgammon is a popular game today, but it is far from modern. Over five thousand years ago, Egyptians played a game called senet. A senet board was one of the objects found in King Tut's tomb. In ancient Rome, senet was replaced by a game known as tables. It was popular throughout Europe during the Middle Ages. Then it evolved into the current game of backgammon.

    A Senet and backgammon are the same game.

    B Games change over the centuries because people change.

    C Backgammon is a classic game resembling a game played in ancient Egypt and ancient Rome.

Check Up

Circle the answer for each question.

1. French fries were actually invented in Belgium. A person from France who visited Belgium tried some of the fried potatoes. He found the treat so tasty he brought the idea back to France with him. Soon the french fry fad spread from Belgium to northern France. In time, french fries became more popular in France than in Belgium.

   French fries are not called Belgian fries because

   A the French are better cooks

   B the French stole the idea from Belgium

   C of the way they are fried

   D they became so much more popular in France

2. The Europeans had never seen corn until Columbus visited the Americas. So, of course, they'd never heard of popcorn. The first Europeans to taste popcorn were the settlers who dined at the first Thanksgiving dinner. It was then that the American Indians showed them how to make it.

   Popcorn is an American food that

   F came from Europe

   G people around the world enjoy

   H was first enjoyed by American Indians

   J not many people know about

3. If airplanes were as germ-ridden as common houseflies, no airport would let them land. Born as squirming maggots, houseflies are one of the world's dirtiest insects. Because they multiply quickly and can travel many miles, they have been a major factor in the spread of diseases.

   Houseflies spread diseases because they

   A carry germs and leave them where they land

   B began as maggots

   C are tiny

   D live in many locations

4. Grazing cows often eat dangerous objects such as nails or wire by accident. To protect their cows from being damaged by these objects, some farmers make them swallow magnets. The magnet is large enough that it stays in the cow's stomach. It attracts and holds any metal objects the cow eats. Then dangerous metal objects don't injure the cow's digestive system.

   The farmers' solution to the problem of cows eating dangerous objects is

   F risky

   G silly

   H practical

   J cruel

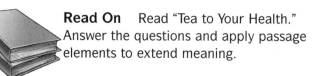

Read On   Read "Tea to Your Health." Answer the questions and apply passage elements to extend meaning.

Review

Predicting Outcomes

When you read and use clues in the story to guess what will probably come next, you are **predicting an outcome**.

Identifying Fact and Opinion

A **fact** is a statement that can be proven.

An **opinion** is someone's idea or belief. An opinion cannot be proved.

> **Fact:** The whale is a mammal.
> **Opinion:** The whale is a fascinating animal.

Recognizing Author's Purpose

An **author's purpose** is the reason why he or she writes. Four common purposes are to inform, to persuade, to describe, and to tell a story.

Recognizing Author's Effect and Intention

Examples of **authors' intentions** are to entertain, inform, persuade, or express feelings. Style techniques like word choices, images, and figurative language reveal tone and help readers identify the **author's effect.**

Making Generalizations

A **generalization** is a conclusion that applies to many people, facts, or situations.

Identifying Style Techniques

Authors use words, details, and types of sentences to create a certain feeling in their writing.

Applying Passage Elements

You can use clues to extend meaning beyond the ideas presented in the passage.

Assessment

Read the paragraphs and circle the answer for each question.

Rodents can infest barns and grain silos where they ruin tons of valuable farm products. Some rodents also carry fleas that can spread diseases to farm animals. But rodents also eat insects and weeds that cause crop damage. Rodents help keep the topsoil rich and fresh by burrowing underground.

1. What generalization can you make from this paragraph?

   A Farmers should keep all rodents away from their farmland.

   B Although rodents can cause crop damage, they also help farmers in several ways.

   C All rodents carry disease to farm animals.

   D Rodents spend all of the time underground.

2. How do rodents improve a farmer's soil?

   F by eating insects

   G by living in fields where crops do not grow

   H by chasing away other animals

   J by borrowing underground

At the beginning of this century, all the rice grown in China was brown. Brown is the natural color of rice. A rice-mill owner found a way to make the grain look white. He made a machine to scrape off the outer brown layers of the rice grains. After all, white rice looks prettier. After the Chinese switched from brown rice to white, thousands of them got sick. They contracted a disease called beriberi. A scientist discovered the cause of beriberi. It was the white rice. The rice's brown shell contains a vitamin. This vitamin is called thiamin, or B_1. Beriberi is caused by the lack of B_1.

3. Which sentence is **not** a fact?

   A Brown is the natural color of rice.

   B After all, white rice looks prettier.

   C After the Chinese switched from brown rice to white, thousands of them got sick.

   D Beriberi is caused by the lack of B_1.

4. What is the author's main purpose?

   F to persuade the reader to eat brown rice

   G to explain how to make white rice

   H to inform the reader about why brown rice is better to eat than white rice

   J to tell the reader about the symptoms of beriberi

I'm driving home from a long day at work. The traffic is heavy. I feel the beginning of a bad headache. I turn the corner. I slam on my brakes. Two teens are in-line skating down the middle of the street.

One is spinning on one skate, like a mad stork. The other is doing some kind of wild dance. They block the whole street with their childish tricks. I sit steaming behind the steering wheel. Meanwhile, these goofs twirl and prance about. They grin and laugh as if they think they were entertaining all the drivers.

5. The short sentences in the first paragraph help to show the speaker's

   A intelligence

   B tense frame of mind

   C relaxed feeling

   D sense of humor

6. Which phrases reveal the speaker's attitude toward the skaters?

   F "a long day at work"

   G "slam on my brakes"

   H "these goofs twirl and prance about"

   J "grin and laugh"

Singing is fun for everyone. But someone has said that you are a monotone or that you sing off-key. Now you think that you can't sing. Don't you believe it. A monotone is a singer who sings everything on one note. If you're a monotone, you have trouble telling the difference between high and low pitches. It doesn't mean that you can't sing different pitches. It only means that you have to learn to do it. Try talking for five minutes without letting your voice go up or down. It will naturally try to vary the pitch. If you put you hand on your neck you can feel your neck muscles work when you talk. You can control the pitch. Your voice can do the same thing when you sing.

7. Which sentence is an opinion?

   A Singing is fun for everyone.

   B It doesn't mean that you can't sing different pitches.

   C It will naturally try to vary the pitch.

   D You can control the pitch.

8. What generalization can you make from this paragraph?

   F Most singers begin as monotones.

   G Most people can learn to control pitch when they sing.

   H To sing well, you must learn to talk in a monotone.

   J Your voice is used differently when talking and singing.

One of the greatest inventions of all times was the railroad. Nothing like it had ever been seen before. The iron road opened up the world to vast numbers of people. Until that time, they had been rooted to their birthplaces. Other forms of travel had been slow, costly, and risky. Now the freedom to travel was there for all to enjoy. Businesspeople all over the world soon understood the importance of railroads. They formed large railroad companies. They did much to attract passengers. 1n 1867 George Pullman organized a company to build a sleeping car. Railroads also introduced luxurious parlor cars and elegant dining service for wealthy travelers.

9. From this paragraph you can generalize that

   A overall, railroad travel was faster, cheaper, and safer than earlier forms of travel

   B railroad travel was designed only for businesspeople

   C people did not like to travel

   D railroads grew slowly throughout the world

10. What is one reason why railroad companies had to be large?

    F Trains were bigger than covered wagons and stagecoaches.

    G Building railroads took hard work from many people and plenty of money.

    H Small numbers of people traveled on trains.

    J Many people wanted to work for the railroad.

11. The tone of this passage is

    A awestruck

    B informative

    C impatient

    D excited

Posttest

Circle the word that is spelled correctly and completes each sentence.

1. The new _____ serves unusual sandwiches.

   A resteraunt

   B restaurant

   C restarant

   D resterant

2. You can count on Kate to finish the job; she is _____.

   F relyable

   G reilable

   H reliable

   J relieble

3. Did you _____ the carpet?

   A vacuum

   B vacume

   C vaccum

   D vaccuum

4. _____ shoes are in the hallway?

   F Who's

   G Whoose

   H Whose

   J Who'se

Circle the answer that is a synonym for each underlined word.

5. the <u>following</u> day

   A previous

   B next

   C soonest

   D second

6. unkind <u>remark</u>

   F comment

   G question

   H joke

   J look

7. <u>guide</u> the boat through the water

   A plow

   B race

   C tow

   D steer

8. <u>end</u> of the story

   F midpoint

   G conclusion

   H theme

   J boundary

9. <u>clutched</u> her purse

   A dangled loosely

   B opened carefully

   C dropped carelessly

   D held tightly

Circle the answer that is an antonym for each underlined word.

10. true statement

    F honest

    G honorable

    H short

    J false

11. purchase a new car

    A buy

    B trade

    C sell

    D drive

12. temperature below freezing

    F behind

    G beneath

    H near

    J above

13. amusing story

    A charming

    B interesting

    C scary

    D distressing

14. major decision

    F minor

    G significant

    H thoughtful

    J impulsive

15. dependable friend

    A unreliable

    B loyal

    C trustworthy

    D likable

Circle the answer to each question.

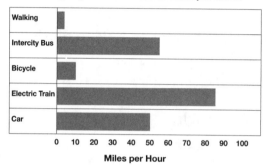

Average Speeds of Kinds of Transportation

16. Which kind of transportation has the greatest average speed per hour?

    F intercity bus

    G bicycle

    H electric train

    J car

17. What is the average speed of a bicycle?

    A 4 mph

    B 10 mph

    C 50 mph

    D 85 mph

Average Annual Precipitation in Missouri

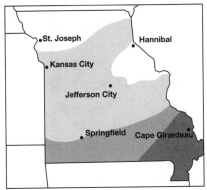

Inches		Centimeters
More than 44		More than 112
40 to 44		102 to 112
36 to 40		91 to 102
Less than 36		Less than 91

Grand Opening Sale!

Pay No Interest till 2002!*

Deluxe Oak TV Center
Special $399—lowest price in town

42" Computer Desk
Holds most 17" monitors
15 at $279 each

88" Leather Sofa
$599—Far below market prices on all leather!

Frank's Furniture Store
125 W. Main
Clark City, IL

Special prices not available on prior orders.
Limited to stock on hand.

*No interest charge until 2007 on purchases over $1,000.

18. Which city gets the greatest amount of precipitation?

  F St. Joseph

  G Springfield

  H Cape Girardeau

  J Hannibal

19. What is the annual average amount of precipitation in St. Joseph?

  A more than 44 inches

  B 40 to 44 inches

  C 36 to 40 inches

  D less than 36 inches

20. Which cities get the same amount of precipitation?

  F St. Joseph and Jefferson City

  G Kansas City and Jefferson City

  H Jefferson City and Cape Girardeau

  J Springfield and St. Joseph

21. This ad tries to catch the consumer's attention by its

  A large selection

  B low prices

  C free delivery policy

  D hassle-free return policy

22. When Tom received his credit card bill for a leather sofa, he noticed that interest had been applied to his outstanding balance. What part of the ad should have alerted Tom to the store's policy on interest?

  F Far below market prices on all leather!

  G Limited to stock on hand.

  H Special prices not available on prior orders.

  J No interest charge until 2007 on purchases over $1,000.

The heart is a muscle. It acts like a pump to push blood through the body's veins and arteries. The human heart is about the size of a fist and weighs less than a pound. It is divided into two sections, and each section has a different job. The right side takes blood from the body's veins. Blood that passes through this side of the heart has been used by the body. It contains a waste product called carbon dioxide. The right side pumps the blood to the lungs where the carbon dioxide is removed and oxygen is added. The left side of the heart then collects the clean blood from the lungs and pumps it back to the body through arteries.

23. This paragraph is about

    A the lungs

    B the makeup of blood

    C the veins and arteries

    D the heart

24. In this paragraph the heart is compared to a

    F muscle

    G fist

    H pump

    J filter

25. From this paragraph you can conclude that

    A supplying the body with blood that has oxygen added to it is the most important function of the heart

    B the right side of the heart works harder than the left side of the heart

    C the heart is a more important organ than the lungs

    D veins and arteries weigh more than one pound

26. To learn more about the heart, which word would you look up first in an index?

    F muscle

    G blood

    H carbon dioxide

    J lungs

27. The tone of this passage is

    A enthusiastic

    B straightforward

    C squeamish

    D discouraged

28. What happens after the carbon dioxide is removed from the blood?

    F The blood comes to the heart from the veins.

    G The heart pumps the blood back through the arteries.

    H The blood passes through the right side of the heart.

    J The right side of the heart pumps the blood to the lungs.

Standing in front of the audience, Lupe looked up from her notes and addressed the audience. "And finally," she said, "I promise that if I am elected president of the student council, I will improve communication between the administration and the students." Lupe has planned these moments ever since she entered school this year. She had been the manager of the softball team and treasurer of her ninth grade class. She worked hard at her studies. She had been involved in many volunteer activities. She had good ideas and the willingness to put them into practice. She had dreamed about winning the election. Now her classmates were ready to vote.

29. What word best describes Lupe?

    A friendly

    B shy

    C hard-working

    D trusting

30. What would you predict Lupe might do as a college student?

    F give up all outside activities to concentrate on her studies

    G decide to study mathematics

    H devote all her time to volunteer activities

    J decide to run for a student body office at her college

31. What office is Lupe running for?

    A treasurer of the ninth-grade class

    B manager of the softball team

    C president of the student council

    D not stated

32. Which sentence below is **not** a fact?

    F Lupe ran for student council president.

    G Communication between the administration and students should improve.

    H Some students work hard at various volunteer activities in school.

    J Lupe dreamed about winning the election.

33. What will be the result if Lupe is elected?

    A She will be ninth-grade class treasurer.

    B She will study hard and get good grades.

    C She will improve student-administration communication.

    D She will volunteer for more activities.

34. When did Lupe enter high school?

    F this year

    G four years ago

    H two years ago

    J not stated

If you ever see an oarfish, it is a sight you will never forget. The creature is one of the strangest fish in the sea. Picture a long (up to 30 feet), skinny, silvery fish that looks like a snake. Add a horse head and a mane that extends the entire length of the fish's body. Then imagine red-tipped spines along the front of the fish that look like poles with flags on top. That's the oarfish. It lives deep in the oceans in both the Atlantic and Pacific Oceans.

35. To tell how strange the oarfish looks, the author uses

   A vague images

   B short sentences

   C a detailed description

   D bad examples

36. The body of the oarfish most closely resembles a

   F flagpole

   G snake

   H horse

   J bird

37. Because oarfish make their homes deep in the ocean they are

   A easy to spot

   B very hungry

   C rarely seen

   D always tired

38. The author's purpose in this passage is

   F to compare oarfish to snakes

   G to explain why oarfish live deep in the oceans

   H to describe what oarfish looks like

   J to predict how oarfish will behave

Answer Key and Evaluation Chart

This posttest has been designed to check your mastery of the reading skills studied. Circle the question numbers that you answered incorrectly and review the practice pages covering those skills. Carefully rework those practice pages to be sure you understand those skills.

Key

1.	B
2.	H
3.	A
4.	H
5.	B
6.	F
7.	D
8.	G
9.	D
10.	J
11.	C
12.	J
13	D
14.	F
15.	A
16.	H
17.	B
18.	H
19.	D
20.	G
21.	B
22.	J
23.	D
24.	H
25.	A
26.	G
27.	B
28.	G
29.	C
30.	J
31.	C
32.	G
33.	C
34.	F
35.	C
36.	G
37.	C
38.	H

Tested Skills	Question Numbers	Practice Pages
synonyms	5, 6, 7, 8, 9	21–24, 25–28
antonyms	10, 11, 12, 13, 14, 15	29–32, 33–36
spelling	1, 2, 3, 4	45–48, 49–52
sequence	28	67–70, 71–74
stated concepts	31	75–78, 79–82
graphs	16, 17	89–92
maps	18, 19, 20	93–96
indexes	26	105–108
consumer materials	21, 22	109–112, 113–116
characters	29	123–126, 127–130
main idea	23	131–134, 135–138
compare and contrast	24	139–142, 143–146
drawing conclusions	25	147–150, 151–154
cause and effect	33	155–158, 159–162
predicting outcomes	30	177–180, 181–184
fact and opinion	32	185–188, 189–192
author's purpose	38	193–196
author's effect and intention	27	197–200
generalizations	36	201–204
style techniques	35	205–208
applying passage elements	37	209–212

Answer Key

Unit 1 Words in Context

Page 19

Physical Fitness: respiratory, exercise, cardiovascular, energy, agility; Healthful Eating: calories, food pyramid, protein, vitamins, fiber; Disease: immunity, allergy, antibodies, bacteria, vaccination
Paragraphs will vary.

Page 20

Sentences will vary. **1.** brunch, **2.** cheeseburger, **3.** motel, **4.** infomercial, **5.** gas, **6.** flu, **7.** photo, **8.** movies

Recognizing Synonyms

Page 21

1. show, **2.** need, **3.** top, **4.** children, **5.** tale, **6.** small, **7.** attempt, **8.** unlock, **9.** brief, **10.** twist, **11.** show, **12.** story, **13.** attempt, **14.** Twist, **15.** need, **16.** open, **17.** tiny, **18.** crest, **19.** youngsters, **20.** brief

Page 22

1. mountains, **2.** Roam, **3.** picked, **4.** melody, **5.** Pursue, **6.** arrives, **7.** go, **8.** females, **9.** majority, **10.** grand

Page 23

Sentences will vary. Possible answers: **1.** He is the greatest magician in the world. **2.** We had a terrific time on our vacation. **3.** These woods are spooky at night. **4.** The polar bear has huge paws. **5.** Could you please help me empty the dishwasher? **6.** The rabbit will hop around the room until it is fed. **7.** Stopping suddenly made me feel dizzy. **8.** Jeff's dog is able to spring over the back fence. **9.** The little boy was shy around all of the adults. **10.** This bug spray will offer protection against the mosquitoes.

Page 24

1. B, **2.** J, **3.** D, **4.** J, **5.** A, **6.** G, **7.** A, **8.** H

Using Synonyms

Page 25

Sentences will vary. **1.** tiny; little; small, **2.** build; construct; make, **3.** grab; take; steal, **4.** devour; eat; dine, **5.** correct; right; proper, **6.** arrived; reached; came

Page 26

1. quick, **2.** troubled, **3.** story, **4.** seemed, **5.** rose, **6.** serious, **7.** vanished, **8.** respect, **9.** constant, **10.** vent

Page 27

Sentences will vary.
Possible answers: **1.** The explorers were looking for a water route through the Americas. **2.** The boats sailed into the harbor. **3.** The sandbars are in shallow waters. **4.** The rich woman gives money to the museum. **5.** The canal connected the river to the sea. **6.** She purchased the tickets yesterday. **7.** Did you help repair the car? **8.** We are currently in the first quarter of the year. **9.** The new rule will permit workers to wear casual clothes on Fridays. **10.** I would like to go to Egypt some day.

Page 28

1. C, **2.** F, **3.** D, **4.** G, **5.** B, **6.** J, **7.** C, **8.** G

Recognizing Antonyms

Page 29

1. C, **2.** E, **3.** H, **4.** G, **5.** A, **6.** F, **7.** I, **8.** B, **9.** J, **10.** D, **11.** Southern, **12.** old, **13.** destroyed, **14.** everyone, **15.** cold, **16.** noisy

Answer Key continued

Page 30
1. give, 2. horrible, 3. friend, 4. throw,
5. entertaining, 6. lead, 7. wrap, 8. thick,
9. listen, 10. doubt

Page 31
Sentences will vary. Possible answers:
1. The cup is empty. 2. The crew
uniforms are all alike. 3. Tiny white
flowers covered the bushes. 4. The lot
was so crowded that there was nowhere
to park. 5. Daisies are common garden
flowers. 6. The ceiling had been painted
sky blue. 7. Never use appliances near
water. 8. The fewest number of people
attended that session. 9. The outspoken
man offered his opinion to anyone who
would listen. 10. Plants will die without
water.

Page 32
1. B, 2. J, 3. C, 4. G, 5. B, 6. G, 7. D, 8. H

Using Antonyms

Page 33
1. near, 2. to, 3. together, 4. right, 5. often,
6. started, 7. never, 8. find, 9. good,
10. first, 11. last, 12. near, 13. find,
14. apart, 15. wrong, 16. finished,
17. never, 18. good, 19. to

Page 34
1. hard, 2. little, 3. friend, 4. smooth,
5. aware, 6. majority, 7. consider,
8. forget, 9. negative, 10. cause

Page 35
Sentences will vary. Possible answers:
1. The jacket was too small to fit him.
2. The game ended in a tie. 3. The last
person home locked the front door.
4. A blizzard closed all the airports in
the East. 5. Slower traffic stays in the
right lane. 6. We expected to see a tame,
quiet movie. 7. Our new computer is
much faster. 8. She felt worse than she
did the night before. 9. Initially, he was
reluctant to go on the trip. 10. We
enjoyed the music played before the
movie began.

Page 36
1. B, 2. J, 3. C, 4. F, 5. B, 6. H, 7. A, 8. J

Recognizing Context Clues

Page 37
1. tired, 2. a feeling and a place, 3. open
waters that belonged to no nation,
4. made motionless because there is no
wind, 5. stuck, 6. avoid, 7. calm spots,
8. in a slump

Page 38
1. A, 2. F, 3. B, 4. J

Page 39
1. stay in the air without moving their
wings; A, 2. unmotorized plane; F,
3. still and stretched out; C, 4. tiny; F,
5. moving; to rise and stay above; A,
6. impossible; G, 7. windless days; A

Page 40
1. B, 2. G, 3. B, 4. J, 5. A, 6. H

Answer Key continued

Using Context Clues

Page 41
1. pretended, 2. formal dance, 3. strips,
4. put liquid on while cooking,
5. tiny, 6. repeated part

Page 42
1. in contrast to, 2. searched closely,
3. a reference, 4. almost, 5. bother,
6. taken out, 7. a limited period of time,
8. turn down, 9. said no, 10. not good

Page 43
1. ancient animals that looked like hairy
elephants, 2. whole, 3. kept safe,
4. surprised, 5. unfrozen, 6. able to be
eaten, 7. earliest

Page 44
1. B, 2. H, 3. D, 4. F, 5. B, 6. H

Spelling Words

Page 45
1. Whose, 2. they're, 3. It's; its, 4. your,
5. passed, 6. too; to

Page 46
1–5 Words and sentences will vary.

Page 47
1. There, 2. feet, 3. sense, 4. pair, 5. way,
6. hear

Page 48
1. C, 2. G, 3. C, 4. F, 5. B, 6. G, 7. D, 8. G

More Spelling Words

Page 49
1. windier, 2. relative, 3. storage,
4. triumphant, 5. translator, 6. destroyer,
7. stirring, 8. comparable,
9. arrangement, 10. beautiful

Page 50
1. profoundly, 2. luxurious, 3. sleeping,
4. moving, 5. stopped, 6. replacing,
7. successful, 8. Unfortunately,
9. carried, 10. burial

Page 51
1. campers, 2. safely, 3. moorings,
4. satisfied, 5. roasting, 6. counselor,
7. processed, 8. Obviously

Page 52
1. A, 2. G, 3. B, 4. H, 5. D, 6. F, 7. C, 8. F

Assessment

Page 54
1. B, 2. F, 3. C, 4. F, 5. A, 6. G, 7. D, 8. H,
9. C, 10. J, 11. C, 12. J, 13. C, 14. H, 15. A,
16. J, 17. B, 18. H

Unit 2 Recalling Information

Page 57

1. broil, **2.** Brush one side with oil.
3. Drain and mash them. **4.** olive oil,
5. 6

Page 58

1. K, **2.** D, **3.** Q, **4.** G, **5.** A, **6.** L, **7.** B,
8. T, **9.** E, **10.** S, **11.** R, **12.** C, **13.** O, **14.** F,
15. H, **16.** I, **17.** N, **18.** J, **19.** P, **20.** M

Recognizing Details

Page 59

1. Answers will vary. Possible answer:
Metal conducts heat and shouldn't be
used for handles on pots and pans.
2. Metal gets hot very quickly. It gets
hot and stays hot.

Page 60

1. B, **2.** J, **3.** B, **4.** J

Page 61

1. D, **2.** F, **3.** B, **4.** G

Page 62

1. B, **2.** F, **3.** B, **4.** G

Recalling Details

Page 63

1. Answers will vary. Possible answers:
Unusual weather causes it to rain fish in
Australia; A strange rain sometimes
falls over northern Australia. **2.** Possible
answer: Tornadoes cause strong
whirlwinds to form above the sea.
These winds are so strong that they can
lift water, seaweed, and driftwood.
They can even lift whole schools of fish
from the water. Fish are carried inland
and then fall from the sky.

Page 64

1. Answers will vary. Possible answers:
Useful Cowhand Wear; Handy Western
Clothes, **2.** Answers will vary. Possible
answers: Boots have pointed toes and
high heels. The heels on boots keep the
boots from sliding through the stirrups
and throwing the cowhand off-balance.
Hats have wide brims to shade the
cowhand's face and neck. A bandanna,
or neckerchief, absorbs sweat. When the
wind raises dust, the cowhand reties the
cloth around the nose and mouth to
keep out the dust. **3.** Answers will vary.
Possible answer: encyclopedia,
nonfiction book

Page 65

1–2 Answers will vary.
Possible answers: The gold rush took
place in the Klondike. Many
prospectors lived in Dawson in 1898.
3–4 Answers will vary. Possible
answers: Milk sold for sixteen dollars a
gallon. Eggs sold for three dollars a
dozen. **5.** Answers will vary. Possible
answer: Grocers made more money
than some gold prospectors in the
Klondike. **6.** Answers will vary. Possible
answers: Monkeys use their tails to
swing from branch to branch. Cows use
their tails to keep insects away. Fish use
their tails to swim. Foxes use their tails
to keep warm.

Page 66

1. C, **2.** H, **3.** C, **4.** H

Answer Key continued

Recognizing Sequence

Page 67
1. A, **2.** F, **3.** D, **4.** First; Next; Then; After; Finally

Page 68
1. A, **2.** J, **3.** B, **4.** G

Page 69
Steps: The Life Cycle of a Wasp 1. They separate the sections of the nest with grass, stone, or mud. **2.** The queen lays eggs. **3.** The workers take care of the eggs. **4.** They feed the baby wasps. **5.** The young wasps grow up and learn to fly.

Steps: Obtaining a Patent
1. The inventor records the date the invention came to mind. **2.** The inventor draws a sketch with a description of the idea. **3.** The inventor has two witnesses sign the document. **4.** The inventor pays a filing fee and submits an application. **5.** The patent office checks to see if anyone else has a patent for the same invention. **6.** If the application is accepted, the patent office gives the invention a number.

Page 70
1. C, **2.** F, **3.** D, **4.** H

Understanding Sequence

Page 71
1. 3, **2.** 2, **3.** 8, **4.** 5, **5.** 1, **6.** 10, **7.** 4, **8.** 7, **9.** 6, **10.** 9

Page 72
1. Ana and Lee picked the apples.
2. They delivered flyers after picking the apples and making the signs. **3.** Ana and Lee set the fruit on a table in the front yard. **4.** No. They ate all the apples before the first shopper stopped. **5.** Lee crosses the street to say good-bye.

Page 73
1. make a hole in the tree and put a spout in the hole, **2.** in the late winter or early spring, **3.** They were emptied into storage barrels. **4.** when enough water had boiled away, **5.** It was passed through a flannel strainer.

Page 74
1. B, **2.** G, **3.** D, **4.** H

Recognizing Stated Concepts

Page 75
1. The gas in your stove has probably traveled a long distance. **2.** That gas is pumped through huge pipelines is the more important concept to remember. The size of the pipelines provides a supporting detail, not an important concept. **3.** Answers will vary but should focus on the process of accessing formation and pumping gas. Possible answer: Gas comes through shafts drilled into the ground. It is pumped through huge pipelines to the gas company. From there it is sent through more pipes to homes.

Page 76
1. not stated, **2.** stated, **3.** stated, **4.** not stated, **5.** stated, **6.** not stated

Page 77
1. Earth's atmosphere causes more rocks from space to burn up before they reach its surface. stated, **2.** Arizona; stated, **3.** brain; stated, **4.** no; not stated

Page 78
1. C, **2.** F, **3.** B, **4.** F

Answer Key continued

Recalling Stated Concepts

Page 79
1. D, 2. G, 3. A, 4. F

Page 80
1. A, 2. G, 3. C, 4. J

Page 81
1. John Adams and Thomas Jefferson died. 2. The paragraph states that they were the second and third presidents of the United States. 3. Thomas Jefferson, 4. grains, 5. Grains have lots of vitamins and fiber.

Page 82
1. A, 2. J, 3. C, 4. G

Assessment

Page 84
1. A, 2. H, 3. B, 4. F, 5. A, 6. G, 7. A, 8. J, 9. D, 10. F, 11. C, 12. G

Unit 3 Graphic Information

Page 87
1. station on the ground
2. communications satellite, 3. to the cable station, 4. through a cable

Page 88
1. Fly to Mexico with my family in January to visit relatives. 2. Save $1300 this year by putting $25 a week into a savings account. 3. Take computer lessons one night a week to learn how to use my computer. 4. Have lunch with my grandfather every Wednesday at a local restaurant. 5. Paint the living room before the family reunion in July. 6. Join the Running Club and exercise on machines twice a week. 7. Answers will vary.

Reading Graphs

Page 89
1. Lengths of U.S. Rivers, 2. the length of a river in miles, 3. counting by five hundreds, 4. Mississippi, 5. Klamath, 6. a boat going down the Snake River

Page 90
1. the Jackson family's expenses, 2. the percentage of expenses spent in each category, 3. housing, 4. transportation, 5. miscellaneous, 6. clothes, 7. 70%

Page 91
1. time, 2. temperature, 3. temperatures at different times, 4. 53°, 5. noon, 6. 9 A.M. and 10 A.M.

Page 92
1. C, 2. J, 3. C, 4. J, 5. A

Reading Maps

Page 93
1. road map, 2. Huntsville, Alabama, 3. north/south, 4. Answers will vary. Possible answers: University of Alabama in Huntsville; U.S. Space and Rocket Center Space Camp; Marshall Space Flight Center, (NASA); U.S. Army Missile Command, 5. Rideout Road, 6. no, 7. McDonald River, 8. about 5 miles or 8 km

Page 94
1. The legend shows export products. 2. North America; South America; Africa; Europe, 3. Africa, 4. Most countries rely on oil/petroleum as a single export. 5. Two countries rely on coffee as a single export. 6. No country in North America relies on a single export.

Answer Key continued

Page 95
1. 1,368 miles, 2. Chicago, 3. 1,271,
4. through Nashville, 5. Charleston;
Washington, D.C.; New York, 6. about
two days, 7. More, because it is 891
miles if you go in a straight line over
the ocean. The land route would be
longer because it isn't a straight line.

Page 96
1. B, 2. J, 3. C, 4. G, 5. D

Using Forms

Page 97
1. Social Security number, 2. Printing is
usually easier to read than cursive
writing. 3. $24,000

Page 98
1. a realistic amount of money that you
would like to be paid, 2. when you
could start working, 3. the year you
graduated from college, 4. in item 7—
Other Education

Page 99
1. the person applying for the insurance,
2. the applicant's husband or wife,
3. Write an estimate and weigh yourself
before submitting the application.
4. circle one of them

Page 100
1. B, 2. G, 3. D

Using Schedules

Page 101
1. morning trains, 2. every 15 minutes,
3. 20 minutes, 4. 6:30 train, 5. 7:12,
6. 7:32, 7. the 6:45 train does not stop
there, 8. 6:30 train

Page 102
1. 7, 2. the program from the previous
time is still running, 3. Baseball's Game
of the Week; Prairie Golf Tournament,
4. Channel 6, 5. *This Year in Politics*,
6. *Patty's Pet Parade; Can't Stop Laughin'*,
7. PBS; WGN; and ESPN, 8. *Kay Winters,
Private Eye; A Tour of China; World
Economy; Meet the Players*

Page 103
1. 2:30 P.M. 2. 2:45 P.M. 3. 22, 4. 123
to Phoenix, 5. 3:15 P.M. 6. 302; 447,
7. 243, 8. Chicago

Page 104
1. A, 2. H, 3. D, 4. J, 5. A

Using Indexes

Page 105
1. pp. 425–431, 444–452, 431–434,
2. African myths and American myths,
3. centaurs, 4. Venus, 5. 313

Page 106
1. true, 2. true, 3. true, 4. false: It's by
Frans Hals. 5. false: Pictures of Chinese
ceramics are on p. 57. There are no
pictures of African ceramics on p. 925.

Page 107
1. September, 2. three, 3. p. 56,
4. "Microprocessors in 2020." 5. August,
6. Kay Redfield Jamison

Page 108
1. C, 2. J, 3. A, 4. J, 5. C, 6. G, 7. C, 8. H

Answer Key continued

Understanding Consumer Materials

Page 109

1. wireless phone service, 2. because there are so many minutes available if you take this offer, 3. to look for information in small print about conditions for this offer, 4. The advertiser wants to draw your attention to them. 5. The advertiser is required to put the information in the ad but doesn't want it to be something you focus on.

Page 110

1. pay the balance in full within a year from the date of purchase, 2. because it catches readers' attention and perhaps leads them to read the rest of the ad, 3. The offer is only good if you have a good credit rating. 4. because they make money when you use their credit plan, 5. yes, because more than a year has passed since the purchase was made

Page 111

1. that if you buy this book you will get rich, 2. they will go from being losers to being winners, 3. people who aren't satisfied with the amount of money they are making, 4. The company is trying to get readers to buy the product quickly. 5. No, the ad never states that as a fact. 6. Find a copy in the library or a bookstore and review it first.

Page 112

1. B, 2. F, 3. B, 4. H

Using Consumer Materials

Page 109

1. The Lessee is the person who is renting the apartment. 2. No. The lease specifically states that the apartment can only be used as a residence. 3. $1,500 security deposit, 4. A penalty of $100 is added to the amount owed. 5. No. The rent would be only four business days late. 6. when the lease ends

Page 114

1. money owed on other credit cards that will be put on this new card, 2. 3.9%, 3. Answers will vary. Possible answer: The chart contains the details of the percentage rate and other charges; it is not information the credit card company wants the reader to focus on. 4. asterisk, or star, 5. 13.9%

Page 115

1. The LOW indicator flashes. 2. to maintain its ability to recharge fully, 3. by leaving the handset off the base until the LOW indicator flashes, 4. The battery pack and the AC adapter may not be connected properly, or the charging contacts may be dirty. 5. Clean the charging contacts on the base and handset with a pencil eraser.

Page 116

1. C, 2. F, 3. B, 4. H

Assessment

Page 118: 1. B, 2. G, 3. C, 4. H, 5. B, 6. F, 7. A, 8. G, 9. D, 10. H, 11. C, 12. J, 13. B, 14. H, 15. C, 16. J, 17. A, 18. G

Answer Key continued

Unit 4 Constructing Meaning

Page 121
Answers will vary.

Page 122
Answers will vary.

Recognizing Character Traits

Page 123
1. D, **2.** H, **3.** A, **4.** G

Page 124
1. shy, **2.** friendly, **3.** ambitious,
4. annoying

Page 125
Answers will vary.
Possible answers: **1.** Tonya is hard-working, thrifty, and giving. **2.** Tim is single-minded and enthusiastic.
3. Clarence is hard-working and talented. **4.** Marisa is caring and unselfish.

Page 126
1. B, **2.** H, **3.** B, **4.** G, **5.** A

Identifying Character Traits

Page 127
1. flat, **2.** dynamic, **3.** dynamic, **4.** flat

Page 128
1. unyielding and stubborn, **2.** self-serving and critical, **3.** whiny and dependent, **4.** uncertain and indecisive

Page 129
1. flat—a nerd, **2.** dynamic—excited and proud of her success, **3.** dynamic—change can be good, **4.** flat—athlete, spends all his time on sports

Page 130
1. B, **2.** J, **3.** A, **4.** G, **5.** A, **6.** H

Recognizing Main Idea

Page 131
1. Ben Jonson is one of England's most famous poets and playwrights. **2.** Many cartoon characters have only four fingers. **3.** Of all birds, the best hunter is the golden eagle. **4.** Arthur L. Nalls built and rode a very small bicycle.

Page 132
1. C, **2.** G, **3.** C

Page 133
Sentences will vary.
Possible answers: **1.** One of the largest pizzas ever made was baked and eaten in Little Rock, Arkansas. **2.** Medinas are Tunisian shopping centers with stores arranged by products they sell. **3.** Your foot falls asleep when the flow of blood from the leg is slowed.

Page 134
1. C, **2.** H, **3.** A, **4.** J, **5.** C

Identifying the Main Idea

Page 135
1. Whales are mammals that come to the surface to breathe. **2.** Sometimes zoo animals need to get away from people. **3.** Minerals in hair may show how smart a person is. **4.** The original king of beasts, however, was *Tyrannosaurus rex*, a huge meat-eating dinosaur.

Page 136
1. Many chemicals make up the human body. C, **2.** Humans share this grasping reflex with monkeys. G, **3.** Alfred Hitchcock has been called the master of suspense films. A

Answer Key continued

Page 137
Answers will vary. Possible answers:
1. The California condor is in danger of becoming extinct. **2.** A rattlesnake has a venomous bite but doesn't generally harm people. **3.** Two teenagers once built a bridge themselves to stop their town's argument.

Page 138
1. B, **2.** F, **3.** C

Comparing and Contrasting

Page 139
1. contrast; <u>but,</u> **2.** contrast; <u>however,</u> **3.** compare; <u>Like,</u> **4.** compare; <u>both/and,</u> **5.** compare; <u>as well as,</u> **6.** contrast; <u>on the other hand,</u> **7.** contrast; <u>in contrast,</u> **8.** contrast; <u>unlike,</u> **9.** compare; <u>similarly,</u> **10.** compare; <u>in the same way</u>

Page 140
1. as, **2.** Both/and, **3.** in the same way, **4.** likewise or similarly, **5.** Unlike, **6.** Although, **7.** on the other hand or however, **8.** however

Page 141
Answers will vary. Possible answers:
1. Both broccoli and cauliflower are vegetables. Broccoli is green, but cauliflower is white. **2.** Like Independence Day, Memorial Day is a national holiday. Memorial Day honors military personnel who died for their country; on the other hand, Independence Day celebrates the independence of our country. **3.** A rose loves sun, as does a daisy. Unlike the daisy, a rose has a rich, sweet smell. **4.** People use both ballpoint pens and pencils to write. A pencil makes marks with graphite in contrast to a ballpoint pen which uses ink. **5.** Like a tornado, a hurricane is a destructive storm with high winds. A hurricane develops over water; in contrast, a tornado develops over land. **6.** Both your parents and grandparents love you. However, your parents must discipline you, while your grandparents often may spoil you.

Page 142
1. C, **2.** F, **3.** C, **4.** H, **5.** D, **6.** G

Using Comparison and Contrast

Page 143
Alike: Earth and Venus are about the same size. Venus and Earth have clouds. Venus and Earth have about the same mass and density. Different: Earth has abundant life and water while Venus is too hot for life to develop. Earth's atmosphere contains oxygen while Venus's atmosphere has sulfuric acid.

Page 144
1. Alike: four legs, fur covered; Different: related to wolves, ability to climb trees, **2.** Alike: is a green plant, has spreading roots; Different: has a smooth, simple leaf, has a yellow bloom, **3.** Alike: their uses, materials used to make them; Different: their shapes; how they cover the fingers, **4.** Alike: lives in water, breathes with gills; Different: size, color, **5.** Alike: has equally spaced steps, is a way of moving up and down; Different: is movable, situations in which it is used, **6.** Alike: rhythm, rhyme, stanzas; Different: set to music

Page 145
Answers will vary. Possible answers:
1. The Rocky Mountains and Appalachian Mountains both are located in North America. The Appalachians are gently rounded and worn by time; in contrast, the younger Rocky Mountains are tall with sharp peaks. **2.** Like a fly, an ant is an insect with six legs. Unlike the fly, an ant has no wings and lives in an organized community. **3.** A dance class and an aerobics class both require people to move through a set of steps together. People take a dance class to learn dance steps for pleasure; on the other hand, aerobics students want to get fit. **4.** Like the spoon, the fork is an eating tool. A spoon has a bowl on the end; however, a fork has sharp tines to spear food.

Page 146
1. B, **2.** J, **3.** C, **4.** F, **5.** B

Drawing Conclusions

Page 147
1. Robots are not living. **2.** Since a wooden chair is made from a tree that once was alive, it has cells. **3.** Without sunlight, plants would die, and without food, animals would die. **4.** Therefore, rocks are not living things.

Page 148
1. C, **2.** C, **3.** B

Page 149
Answers will vary. Possible answers:
1. birds' bodies are beautifully adapted for flight, **2.** baby birds must practice and work hard to learn to fly, **3.** the shape and size of the wing affects the bird's ability to fly

Page 150
1. D, **2.** G, **3.** C, **4.** F

More Drawing Conclusions

Page 151
1. true, **2.** false, *circle:* A mouse is a sparrow. A mouse has feathers. **3.** false, *circle:* Rags is a person. **4.** true, **5.** false, *circle:* All two-legged animals are human. An ostrich is human. **6.** true

Page 152
1. A, **2.** B, **3.** B, **4.** A, **5.** A, **6.** B, **7.** B, **8.** B

Page 153
Answers will vary. Possible answers:
1. The collie is descended from wild ancestors. **2.** The mosquito that bit me was a female. **3.** A rabbit gnaws on hard things to wear down its teeth. **4.** The word *chrysanthemum* has four syllables. **5.** Only cats purr. **6.** All horses have hooves.

Page 154
1. C, **2.** F, **3.** B, **4.** H, **5.** B

Recognizing Cause and Effect

Page 155
1. yes, **2.** yes, **3.** no, **4.** no, **5.** *underline:* Since, *circle:* injuries from scooter accidents have risen, **6.** *underline:* therefore, *circle:* I now have a B average in science, **7.** *underline:* Because, *circle:* we were late for our first class, **8.** *underline:* as a result, *circle:* several small shops downtown lost business and failed

Answer Key continued

Page 156
1. therefore, thus, as a result, or consequently; *underline:* I have gained weight, **2.** Because or Since; *underline:* I could not get into the house, **3.** If/then; *underline:* you cannot win it, **4.** so that; *underline:* I would not have to fuss with it constantly, **5.** as a result, thus, therefore, or consequently; *underline:* she earns a lot of money, **6.** because; *underline:* Juney has to follow a strict diet, **7.** because or since; *underline:* The ducklings followed me everywhere, **8.** as a result, consequently, thus, or therefore; *underline:* our grass is thick and green, **9.** If/then; *underline:* we will hold the house for you, **10.** due to; *underline:* Farmers have not finished planting their crops

Page 157
Answers will vary. Possible answers:
1. Because I dropped the phone, I can't get a dial tone. **2.** Megan slipped and fell on a concrete floor; as a result, she broke her wrist. **3.** If it rains more than six inches in a day, then the river will rise and flood the town. **4.** Interest rates rose dramatically; consequently, sales of homes fell. **5.** Because health care has improved, more people are living longer. **6.** American families move more often now than in the past; as a result, children must change schools more often. **7.** Since the cost of living has skyrocketed, most families need two wage earners. **8.** The dog's tail hit the vase, so the vase fell and broke.

Page 158
1. C, **2.** F, **3.** D, **4.** G

Identifying Cause and Effect

Page 159
1. Circle the first three sentences. Box the last sentence. **2.** Circle the first sentence. Box the last three sentences.

Page 160
1. Causes: The days grew short. The weather turned colder. Effect: The geese flew south. **2.** Cause: The furnace stopped working. Effects: The pipes in the house froze. The houseplants died. **3.** Cause: Heavy rain flooded the town. Effects: Houses were destroyed. Drinking water was scarce. People were evacuated.

Page 161
Answers will vary. Possible answers:
1. The female chooses a male as a mate.
2. The final bell for the school day rings.
3. You feel good and are physically fit.

Page 162
1. C, **2.** H, **3.** A, **4.** F, **5.** D, **6.** J

Summarizing and Paraphrasing

Page 163
1. paraphrase; summary, **2.** summary; paraphrase

Page 164
1. C, **2.** G

Answer Key continued

Page 165
Answers will vary. Possible answers:
Paraphrase: The eardrum is a thin flap of skin inside the ear. It vibrates when sound hits it. It sends the vibrations on to three tiny bones that lie behind it. The moving bones cause liquid in a canal to shake. The moving liquid makes nerve cells send impulses to the brain. The brain senses the impulses as sound.
Summary: We hear because the eardrum, bones, and fluid behind them vibrate from sound waves. The vibration stimulates nerve endings in the fluid to send a message to the brain.

Page 166
1. C, **2.** F, **3.** B, **4.** J, **5.** A

Using Supporting Evidence
Page 167
1. A, B, D, and E, **2.** F, G, H, and J

Page 168
1. Test animals go blind, lose fur, and develop tumors. Thousands of animals die each year, but only a few new drugs are produced. Test animals are imprisoned and do not live a natural life. Animals have rights just as people do, but they cannot speak for themselves. **2.** New drugs are needed to save people's lives. Researchers give test animals clean, safe places to live and plenty to eat. Test animals would die sooner in the wild or as homeless strays. No one can prove that these animals actually suffer pain like people do.

Page 169
Answers will vary. Possible answers:
1. A High school students need ways to show their individuality so they can develop as people. **B** Personal style is important to teenagers. **C** Clothing is a harmless way of calling attention to yourself. **2. A** Studies show that people with pets are happier and healthier than those without pets. **B** Pets would give residents something to love that would love them back. **C** Pets provide companionship, and many residents get very few visitors.

Page 170
1. D, **2.** G, **3.** A, **4.** H

Assessment
Page 172
1. B, **2.** F, **3.** C, **4.** H, **5.** C, **6.** G, **7.** C, **8.** F, **9.** D, **10.** H, **11.** D

Unit 5 Extending Meaning
Page 175
1–3 Answers will vary.

Page 176
Sentences will vary.
1. Center City is so small that a cat cannot turn around. **2.** Traffic was so bad that even the tortoise could have fallen asleep. **3.** My friend's cat is so mean she spits instead of purrs. **4.** The subway was so crowded that a sardine can would have seemed roomy. **5.** My uncle's car is in such bad condition that not even mouth-to-mouth resuscitation could save it.

Answer Key continued

Predicting Outcomes

Page 177
1. B, 2. H, 3. B

Page 178
1. C, 2. F, 3. B, 4. H

Page 179
Answers will vary. Possible answers:
1. B, These actions will cool him off and replace lost water. 2. F, She is comfortable there and interested in the work. 3. C, He would find this a more exciting adventure than any other.

Page 180
1. D, 2. F, 3. B, 4. H

More Predicting Outcomes

Page 181
STORY CLUES: Tara wants to "do everything by herself." Adam is on the phone.
EXPERIENCE CLUES: Small children need close supervision. They often don't know what can hurt them.
PREDICTION: Answers will vary. Possible answer: Tara will begin to open the oven, but Adam will get off the phone and stop her from trying to get the trays out.

Page 182
1. B, 2. F, 3. B, 4. F

Page 183
Answers will vary. Possible answers:
1. He will ask her to come to work at the stable for pay. 2. They will eat and play games inside. 3. Beth will probably borrow the sweater without asking.
4. Matt will win the race.

Page 184
1. C, 2. H, 3. C

Recognizing Fact and Opinion

Page 185
1. F, 2. O, 3. O, 4. F, 5. F, 6. F, 7. F, 8. O, 9. F, 10. O

Page 186
1. F, encyclopedia or atlas,
2. F, encyclopedia or atlas,
3. F, encyclopedia, 4. O, 5. O,
6. F, encyclopedia, 7. F, daily newspaper,
8. O

Page 187
1. Today everyone should read a daily paper from first page to last page.
2. Some letters to the editor are ridiculous. 3. You should always check the classified ads so you don't miss the bargains! 4. The funnies are the best part of the whole paper. 5. The new style is much nicer than the old one.

Page 188
1. B, 2. H, 3. D, 4. H, 5. A, 6. J

Answer Key continued

Identifying Fact and Opinion

Page 189
OPINION **1.** Many athletes do a lot of charity work. Many athletes work daily to keep their bodies in shape. Many people are inspired by athletes.
OPINION **2:** Many athletes demand salaries in the millions. Some athletes use illegal drugs. Some athletes get into trouble with the law.

Page 190
1. D, **2.** G, **3.** B, **4.** G, **5.** B

Page 191
1. About 38 percent of 18 to 24 year olds do volunteer work. **2.** Tom Hanks won the academy Award for Best Actor two years in a row. **3.** Eleanor Roosevelt chaired the Human Rights Commission in the 1940s. **4.** About 13 million Americans travel to Canada for fun every year. **5.** Mosquitoes spread diseases such as malaria and encephalitis.

Page 192
1. C, **2.** J, **3.** C, **4.** H

Recognizing Author's Purpose

Page 193
1. describe, **2.** inform or explain, **3.** tell a story, **4.** persuade

Page 194
1. persuade, **2.** inform or explain, **3.** tell a story, **4.** describe, **5.** inform or explain

Page 195
1. B; A, **2.** A; B, **3.** B; A

Page 196
1. B, **2.** J, **3.** A

Recognizing Author's Effect and Intention

Page 197
1. B, **2.** J

Page 198
1. C, **2.** G
Possible answers: **3.** calm, serene, relaxed; **4.** informative; **5.** excited

Page 199
1. C, **2.** F, **3.** D, **4.** H

Page 200
1. B, **2.** F, **3.** D, **4.** G

Making Generalizations

Page 201
1. A, **2.** F

Page 202
1. A, **2.** G, **3.** C, **4.** G

Page 203
Answers will vary.
Possible answers: **1.** is thinking about or playing soccer, **2.** care well for Tuffy, **3.** are around 50 years old, **4.** reads books

Page 204
1. B, **2.** H, **3.** A, **4.** F

Identifying Style Techniques

Page 205
1. B, **2.** F

Page 206
1. C, **2.** G, **3.** C, **4.** G, **5.** A

Page 207
1. A, **2.** G, **3.** A, **4.** H

Page 208
1. A, **2.** H, **3.** A, **4.** G, **5.** D

Applying Passage Elements

Page 209
1. B, 2. F

Page 210
1. A, 2. H, 3. B, 4. H

Page 211
1. A, 2. G, 3. C

Page 212
1. D, 2. H, 3. A, 4. H

Assessment

Page 214
1. B, 2. J, 3. B, 4. H, 5. B, 6. H, 7. A,
8. G, 9. A, 10. G, 11. B